Edwin Arnold

Sir Edwin Arnold was born on 10 June 1832 in Gravesend, Kent, England. He was the second son of a Sussex magistrate, and was educated at King's School Rochester, before moving onto *University College*, Oxford. Arnold won the prestigious Newdigate prize for poetry whilst at Oxford, and soon after graduating became a schoolmaster at *King Edward's School*, Birmingham. From here, he travelled to India in 1856 as Principal of the *Government Sanskrit College* at Poona, a post which he held for seven years. This period included the mutiny of 1857, in which Arnold was able to render services for which he was publicly thanked by Lord Elphinstone in the Bombay Council. It was also during this time that Arnold collected material for many of his future works. Returning to England in 1861, he worked as a journalist with the *Daily Telegraph*, a newspaper with which he continued as associate editor for more than forty years, and later as its editor in chief. It was as a poet that Arnold was best known to his contemporaries however. His most famous work, *The Light of Asia*, published in 1879, went through numerous editions in England and America. It is an Indian epic, dealing with the life and teachings of Buddha. Not without its critics, the poem caused controversy amongst Buddhists and Christians alike; some Oriental scholars argued it gave a false impression of Buddhist doctrine, whilst the suggested analogy between Shakyamuni and Jesus offended many devout Christians. In response to this later criticism, Arnold attempted a second narrative poem, in which the central figure was Jesus, entitled *The Light of the World* (1891). This latter work had considerable poetic merit, but lacked the novelty of the earlier poem which gave it much of its attractiveness. Arnold's other principal works were *Indian Song of Songs* (1875), *Pearls of the Faith* (1883), *The Song Celestial* (1885), *With Sadi in the Garden* (1888), *Tiphar's Wife* (1892) and *Adzuma* or, *The Japanese Wife* (1893). Arnold was married three times in his life, sadly widowed twice. He was awarded the star of India in 1877, on the occasion of the proclamation of Queen Victoria of Empress of India, and was knighted in 1888. Arnold died on 24 March, 1904, aged seventy-one.

PEARLS OF THE FAITH.

PREFACE.

It is a custom of many pious Muslims to employ in their devotions a three-stringed chaplet, each string containing thirty-three beads, and each bead representing one of the "ninety-nine beautiful names of Allah," whenever this—among many other religious uses—is made of it. The Korân bids them "celebrate Allah with an abundant celebration," and on certain occasions —such as during the intervals of the Tarâwih night service in Ramadhân—the Faithful pass these ninety-nine beads of the rosary through their fingers, repeating with each "Name of God" an ejaculation of praise and worship. Such an exercise is called *Zikr*, or "remembrance," and the rosary *Masba'hah*.

In the following pages of varied verse I have enumerated these ninety-nine "beautiful names," and appended to each—from the point of view of an Indian Mohammedan—some illustrative legend, tradition, record, or comment, drawn from diverse Oriental sources; occasionally paraphrasing (as closely as possible) from the text of the Korân itself, any particular passage containing the sacred Title, or casting light upon it. In this way it seemed possible to present the general spirit of Islâm under a new and not unacceptable form; since almost every religious idea of the Korân comes up in the long catalogue of attributives. Tender, as well as terrible; lofty in morality, albeit grim and stern in dogma, the "Perspicuous Book" is still, and must always be, replete with interest for Christendom, since, if Islâm was born in the Desert, with Arab Sabæanism for its mother and Judaism for its father, its foster-nurse was Eastern Christianity, and Muhammad's attitude towards Christ, and towards the religion which bears His name, is ever one of profound reverence and grateful recognition. Nor are the differences between the older and younger creed really so great as their similitudes in certain aspects. The soul of Islâm is its declaration of the unity of God: its heart is the inculcation of an absolute resignation to His will. Not more sublime, therefore, in religious history appears the figure of Paul the tent-maker, proclaiming the "Unknown God" at Athens, than that of the camel-driver Muhammad, son of Abdallah and Amînah, abolishing all the idols of the Arabian Pantheon, except their chief—ALLAH TA'ALAH, "God the Most High"—and under that ancient and well-received appellation establishing the oneness of the origin, government, and life of the universe. Thereby that marvellous and gifted Teacher created a vast empire of new belief and new civilization, and prepared a sixth part of humanity for the developments and reconciliations which later times will bring. For Islâm must be conciliated; it cannot be thrust scornfully aside or rooted out. It shares the task of the education of the world with its sister religions, and it will contribute its eventual portion to

> "that far-off divine event,
> Towards which the whole creation moves."

Composed amid Scotch mountains during a brief

summer-rest from politics, and with no library near at hand for references, my book has need to ask indulgence from the learned. It does but aim, however, to suggest (in poetic form) juster thoughts than sometimes prevail of Islâm, of its founder, and of its votaries; employing the language of one among them, and thinking with his thoughts, since this alone permits the necessary sympathy.

I have thus at length finished the Oriental Trilogy which I designed. In my "Indian Song of Songs" I sought to transfer to English poetry a subtle and lovely Sanskrit idyll of the Hindoo theology. In my "Light of Asia" I related the story and displayed the gentle and far-reaching doctrines of that great Hindoo prince who founded Buddhism. I have tried to present here, in the simple, familiar, and credulous, but earnest spirit and manner of Islâm—and from its own points of view—some of the thoughts and beliefs of the followers of the noble Prophet of Arabia.

EDWIN ARNOLD, C.S.I.

GLENGYLE, PERTHSHIRE, SCOTLAND,
September, 1882.

CONTENTS.

NO.		PAGE
1. *ALLAH*		13
2. *Ar-Rahmân* ..... "The Merciful"		15
(The Sinful Angels.)		
3. *Ar-Raheem* ..... "The Compassionate"		17
(Solomon and the Ant.)		
4. *Al-Mâlik* ..... "The King of Kings"		19
(The Sultan and the Potter.)		
5. *Al-Kuddûs* ..... "The Holy One"		22
(God's Name in Heaven.)		
6. *As-Salâm* ..... "The Peace"		24
(The Peace of Paradise.)		
7. *Al-Maumin* ..... "The Faithful"		27
(The Verity of Sayid.)		
8. *Al-Muhaimin* ..... "The Help in Peril"		30
(The Spider and the Dove.)		
9. *Al-Hathim* ..... "The Mighty"		32
(The Throne-Verse.)		
10. *Al-Jabbâr* ..... "The All-Compelling"		33
(Sura 59.)		
11. *Al-Mutakabbir* ..... "The Majestic"		34
(Azar and Abraham.)		
12. *Al-Khalik* ..... "The Creator"		35
(Signs of the Lord.)		
13. *Al-Bari* ..... "The Artificer"		37
(Angels' Wings.)		
14. *Al-Muzawwir* ..... "The Fashioner"		38
(The Making of Man.)		
15. *Al-Ghaffâr* ..... "The Forgiver"		40
(Abraham's Offence.)		
16. *Al-Kahhâr* ..... "The Dominant"		42
(Sura "Of the Cattle.")		

CONTENTS.

NO.			PAGE
17.	*Al-Wahhâb*	"The Bestower" (Ali and the Angels.)	44
18.	*Al-Razzâk*	"The Provider" (Sura "Of the Forenoon.")	49
19.	*Al-Fâtta'h*	"The Opener" (Muhammad's Journey to Heaven.)	50
20.	*Al-'Alim*	"The All-Knower". (The Moakkibât.)	55
21.	*Al-Kabiz*	"The Closer" (Evil Deeds.)	57
22.	*Al-Bâsit*	"The Uncloser" (Good Deeds.)	59
23.	*Al-Khâfiz*	"The Abaser" (Nimrûd and the Gnat.)	62
24.	*Ar-Rafi*	"The Exalter" (Allah's Prophets.)	63
25.	*Al-Muhizz*	"The Honourer" (Sura "Of Imran's Family.")	65
26.	*Al-Muzîl*	"The Leader Astray" (God's Will and Free-will.)	66
27.	*As-Samî'h*	"The All-Hearing" (A Shepherd's Prayer.)	68
28.	*Al-Bazîr*	"The All-Seeing" (Azrael and the Indian Prince.)	71
29.	*Al-Hâkim*	"The Judge of All" (The Last Day.)	73
30.	*Al-Hâdil*	"The Equitable" (Sura "Of Jonas.")	75
31.	*Al-Latîf*	"The Gracious One" (Sura "Of Counsel.")	76
32.	*Al-Khabîr*	"He who is Aware" (Muhammad in the Cemetery.)	77
33.	*Al-Hâlîm*	"The Clement" (The Dharra and the Date-stone.)	78
34.	*Al-'Aziz*	"The Strong" (Sura "Of Al-Akhâf.")	79
35.	*Al-Ghâfir*	"The Pardoner" (Hassan's Slave.)	80
36.	*Ash-Shâkir*	"The Thankful" (Sura "Of Al-Kâuthar.")	82

CONTENTS.

NO.			PAGE
37.	Al-'Alee	"The Exalted"	84
		(Sura "Of the Bee.")	
38.	Al-Kabîr	"The Very Great"	85
		(The Seven Heavens.)	
39.	Al-Hâfiz	"The Preserver"	87
		(Sura "Of the Night Star.")	
40.	Al-Mukît	"The Maintainer"	88
		(Sura "Of the Inevitable.")	
41.	Al-Hasîb	"The Reckoner"	90
		(Sura "Of Women.")	
42.	Al-Jamîl	"The Beneficent"	91
		(The Rose-Garden.)	
43.	Al-Karîm	"The Bountiful"	93
		(Sura "Of Cleaving Asunder.")	
44.	Al-Rakîb	"The Watchful"	94
		(The Books of Good and Evil.)	
45.	Al-Mujîb	"The Hearer of Prayer"	96
		(Ali and the Jew.)	
46.	Al-Was'ih	"The All-Comprehending"	100
		(Turning to Mecca.)	
47.	Al-Hâkim al Mutlak	"The Judge of Judges"	101
		(The Angels of the Scales.)	
48.	Al-Wadood	"The Loving"	103
		(Tasmîn and Salsabîl.)	
49.	Al-Majîd	"The All-Glorious"	106
		(Sura "Of the Cow.")	
50.	Al-Bâhith	"The Raiser from Death"	107
		(Iblîs and Abraham.)	
51.	Ash-Shahîd	"The Witness"	110
		(Poets and Prophets.)	
52.	Al-Hakk	"The Truth"	111
		(The Sin of Sins.)	
53.	Al-Wakîl	"The Guardian"	112
		(Sura "Of the Cow.")	
54.	Al-Kawi	"The Almighty"	113
		(The Fly and the False Gods.)	
55.	Al-Mateen	"The Firm"	114
		(The Tent-Pole.)	
56.	Al-Walî	"The Nearest Friend"	115
		(Abraham's Bread.)	
57.	Al-Hamîd	"The All-Praiseworthy"	119
		(The Garden and the Rock.)	

NO.			PAGE
58.	Al-Múhsi	"The Accountant"	120
		(Sura "Of the Earthquake.")	
59.	Al-Mubdî	"The Beginner"	121
		(The Light of Life.)	
60.	Al-Mu'hîd	"The Restorer"	122
		(A Message from the Dead.)	
61.	Al-Mo'hyî	"The Quickener"	125
		(Sura "Of the Signs.")	
62.	Al-Mumît	"The Slayer"	126
		(The Angel of Death.)	
63.	Al-Haiy	"The Ever-Living"	129
		(The Life Beyond.)	
64.	Al-Kaiyûm	"The Self-Subsisting"	130
		(The Trumpet.)	
65.	Al-Wâjid	"The All-Perceiving"	131
		(Sura "Of Daybreak.")	
66.	Al-Wâhid	"The One"	133
		(Al-I'hlâs.)	
67.	As-Samad	"The Eternal"	134
		(Ozair the Jew.)	
68.	Al-Kadar	"Providence"	138
		(Kismat.)	
69.	Al-Muktadir	"The All-Powerful"	139
		(Sura "Of the Moon.")	
70.	Al-Mukaddim	"The Forewarner"	140
71.	Al-Muwakhir	"The Fulfiller"	
		(Sura "Of K.")	
72.	Al-Awwal	"The First"	142
73.	Al-Akhir	"The Last"	
74.	Ath-Thâhir	"The Manifest"	
75.	Al-Bâtin	"The Hidden"	
		(The "Mothers of the Names.")	
76.	Al-Wâlî	"The All-Governing"	144
		(Solomon's Signet.)	
77.	Al-Mutâhâli	"The One above Reproach"	149
		(Moses and the Angel.)	
78.	Al-Barr	"The Good"	151
		(The Adulteress.)	
79.	Al-Tawwâb	"The Relenting"	154
		(Adam quitting Eden.)	
80.	Al-Muntakim	"The Avenger"	156
81.	Al-Ghafoor	"The Rewarder"	
		(Hell and Heaven.)	

CONTENTS. 11

NO.			PAGE
82.	*Al-Rawûf*	"The Ever-Indulgent"	160
	(Sura "Of the Star.")		
83.	*Málik-ul-Mulki*	"King of the Kingdom"	162
	(Sura "Of the Emigration.")		
84.	*Dhu'l jalâl wa Ikrâm.*	"Lord of Splendid Power"	163
	(Sura "Of the Merciful.")		
85.	*Al-Muksit*	"The Equitable"	164
	(The Last Sermon of the Prophet.)		
86.	*Al-Jami'h*	"The Gatherer"	167
	(Sura "Of Women.")		
87.	*Al-Ghanî*	"The All-Sufficing"	168
	(Sura "Of Troops.")		
88.	*Al-Mughnî*	"The Sufficer"	170
	(Sura "Of the Afternoon.")		
89.	*Al-Mu'hti*	"The Provider"	171
90.	*Al-Mâni'h*	"The Withholder"	
	(The Two Gateways.)		
91.	*An-Nâfi'h*	"The Propitious"	173
	(The Dove.)		
92.	*Az-Zarr*	"The Harmful"	175
	(King Sheddâd's Paradise.)		
93.	*An-Noor*	"The Light"	181
	(Sura "Of Light.")		
94.	*Al-Hâdî*	"The Guide"	182
	(The Four Travellers.)		
95.	*Al-Azali*	"Eternal in the Past"	184
96.	*Al-Bâkî*	"Eternal in the Future"	
	(Sura "Of Ya Sin.")		
97.	*Al-Warith*	"The Inheritor"	186
	(The Rose and the Dewdrop.)		
98.	*Al-Raschîd*	"The Unerring"	188
	(The Prophet's Oath.)		
99.	*Az-Zaboor*	"The Patient"	190
	(Islâm.)		
NOTES			191

1

"Allah!" Bi-'smi-'llah! Say that God is One, Living, Eternal; and besides Him none.

2

Say Ar-Rahmân! " The Merciful" Him call ;
For He is full of mercy unto all.

ONCE on a day, in Paradise,
Discourse indignant did arise
Amongst the Angels, seeing how
The sons of Adam sinned below;
Albeit Allah's grace had sent
Prophets with much admonishment.
"Heedless and guilty race," they cried,
"Whose penitence is set aside
At each temptation! Truth and Right
Ye know not!"' Then a wondrous light
Fell on their brows—a mighty word
Sounded—the Presence of the Lord
Spake: "Of your number choose ye two
To go among mankind and do
'Justice and Right,' teaching them these."
Therewith, from those bright companies,
Harût went and Marût went down
On earth, laying aside their crown
Of rays, and plumes of rainbow feather;
And on the judgment-seat together
Many long years they sate, and wrought
Just judgment upon each cause brought.

Until, before that justice-seat
There came a woman, fair and sweet,
So ravishing of form and mien
That great Soharah, who is queen
Of the third planet, hath not eyes
As soft, nor mouth made in such wise.
And one whom she did wrong, besought
Sentence against her: she had nought
Of plea, but in her dazzling grace
Stood fearless in the audience-place;
Consuming hearts with hot desire
By subtle Beauty's searching fire.
Then said Hârut, forgetting Heaven,
"Pardon to such must, sure, be given."
Whispered Mârut, "If thou wilt be
Leman of mine, thou shalt go free."
And for her love those two contended,
Till the false scene was sorely ended
With earthquake, and with lightning-flash,
And rolling thunder's wrathful crash,
"Midst which the city and the folk
Passed from their ken, and a Voice spoke:
"Come unto judgment, ye who called
Allah too merciful!"
     Appalled
Harût lay and Marût lay prone
In Paradise, before the Throne;
Hearing that doom of God, which said:
"Until My trumpet calls the dead,
Dwell on the earth, where ye have learned
The just may unto sin be turned."

Merciful One and just! we bless
Thy name, and crave forgiveness.

3

Say Ar-Raheem! call Him "Compassionate,"
For He is pitiful to small and great.

'TIS written that the serving-angels stand
Beside God's throne, ten myriads on each hand,
Waiting, with wings outstretched and watchful eyes,
To do their Master's heavenly embassies.
Quicker than thought His high commands they read,
Swifter than light to execute them speed;
Bearing the word of power from star to star
Some hither and some thither, near and far.
And unto these nought is too high or low,
To mean or mighty, if He wills it so;
Neither is any creature, great or small,
Beyond His pity; which embraceth all,
Because His eye beholdeth all which are;
Sees without search, and counteth without care,
Nor lies the babe nearer the nursing-place
Than Allah's smallest child to Allah's grace;
Nor any ocean roll so vast that He
Forgets one wave of all that restless sea.

Thus it is written; and moreover told
How Gabriel, watching by the Gates of gold,
Heard from the Voice Ineffable this word
Of two-fold mandate uttered by the Lord:
"Go earthward! pass where Solomon hath made
His pleasure-house, and sitteth there arrayed,

Goodly and splendid—whom I crowned the king—
For at this hour My servant doth a thing
Unfitting: out of Nisibis there came
A thousand steeds with nostrils all a-flame
And limbs of swiftness, prizes of the fight;
Lo! these are led, for Solomon's delight,
Before the palace, where he gazeth now
Filling his heart with pride at that brave show;
So taken with the snorting and the tramp
Of his war-horses, that Our silver lamp
Of eve is swung in vain, Our warning Sun
Will sink before his sunset-prayer's begun;
So shall the people say, 'This king, our lord,
Loves more the long-maned trophies of his sword
Than the remembrance of his God?' Go in!
Save thou My faithful servant from such sin."

"Also, upon the slope of Arafat,
Beneath a lote-tree which is fallen flat,
Toileth a yellow ant who carrieth home
Food for her nest, but so far hath she come
Her worn feet fail, and she will perish, caught
In the falling rain; but thou, make the way naught,
And help her to her people in the cleft
Of the black rock."
                Silently Gabriel left
The Presence, and prevented the king's sin,
And holp the little ant at entering in.

O Thou whose love is wide and great,
We praise Thee, " The Compassionate."

4

*Call Him " Al-Mâlik," King of all the kings,
Maker and Master of created things.*

The Sultan of Damascus found asleep
    The potter Ebn Solûl,
And bore him to the palace, where he waked
    In garments beautiful.

  .   .   .   .

Consider! if a king should call thee "friend,"
    And lead thee to his court,
Roofed large with lazulite, and pavemented
    With flow'rs, on green floors wrought;

If he should bid thee sit at meat; and spread
    A table, served so fine
There lacked not any pleasant food or fruit
    But came at call of thine;

If he hung high a glorious golden lamp
    To shine where thy feet tread;
And stretched black 'broidered hangings, sown with gems,
    For curtains to thy bed;

If for thy heats he bade soft zephyrs blow;
    Sent, at thy thirst, sweet rains;
And filled the groves with minstrels, gayly garbed,
    To charm thee with their strains;

If, past the confines of his palace-grounds,
    He showed thee spacious seas,
Where, wafted o'er the dancing foam, might sail
    Thou and thine argosies;

If, for society in that fair place,
    He gave glad companies,
Kinsmen and friends and helpmates, and the bliss
    Of beauty's lips and eyes;

With wisdom's scroll to study, and the ways
    Of wondrous living things;
And lovely pleasure of all ornaments
    That Nature's treasure brings,

Coral and pearl; turkis, and agate stones
    Milk-white or rosy-veined;
Amber and ivory; jade; shawls wove with gold,
    Scarves with sea-purple stained;

If the king gave thee these, and only wrote
    Upon his inner door:
"Serve me and honor me and keep my laws,
    And thus live evermore

In better bliss, when ye shall pass hereby,—
    As surely pass ye must:—"
Who is there would not praise that monarch's name
    With forehead in the dust?

    .   .   .   .

Lo! but He doeth this—Allah our King,
    His sky is lazulite;
His earth is paved with emerald-work; its stores
    Are spread for man's delight;

His sun by day, His silver stars by night,
  Shine for our sakes, His breeze
Cools us and wafts our ships; His pleasant lands
  Are girdled with the seas

Which send the rain, and make the crystal bridge
  Whereby man roams at will
From court to court of Allah's pleasure-house;
  Seeing that writing still

Upon the inner gate—which all must pass—
  "Love me and keep my laws
That ye may live, since there is greater life
  Beyond these darkened doors."

    .   .   .   .

If Ebn Solûl, the potter, loved Him not
  Whose kindness was so strong;
If Ebn Solûl kept not the palace laws,
  Had not that Sultan wrong?

O Sovereign Giver of good things,
We praise Thee, " Málik," King of kings.

5

*Allah-al-Kuddûs—the " Holy One" He is;
But purify thy speech, pronouncing this;*

For even Israfil,
Who waits in Heaven still
Nearest the Throne, and hath the voice of sweetness,
Before his face doth fold
The wings of feathered gold,
Saying "Al-Kuddûs;" and in supreme completeness

Of lowly reverence stands,
Laying his angel-hands
Over his lips, lest Allah's holiest name
Be lightly breathed on high;
And that white mystery
Pass, as if that and others were the same.

* Iblîs—'tis written—when
He heareth among men
The name of "Allah" spoken, shrinks and flies;
But at the sound of this,
Uttered in realms of bliss,
The Djins and Angels, in their ranks, arise.

And what believer dares
Begin his morning prayers

---

*Cf. Korân, cxiv. chapter "Of men."

Without "wuzu'h"—th' ablution? who is seen
        His Korân to rehearse
        But hath in mind its verse,
"Let none me touch, save such as are made clean?"

        Lo! if with streams or sands
        Ye lave the earnest hands
Lifted in prayer; and if ye wash the mouth
        Which reads the sacred scroll,
        Dare ye with sullied soul
Meditate this dread word, that shrines the truth

        Of Allah's purity?
        Bethink! His great eyes see
The hearts of men unto their inmost core!
        Make clean your hearts within;
        Cast forth each inmost sin;
Then with bowed brows, say this name, and adore.

Forgive, Thou Pure One!—Whom we bless—
Of our good deeds the sinfulness.

6

*Thou Who art "Peace," and unto peace dost bring,
Allah-as-Salâm! we praise Thee, Judge and King!*

WHEN th' unshunnĕd Day arriveth, none of men shall
doubt it come;
Into Hell some it will lower, and exalt to Heaven
some.

When the earth with quakenings quaketh, and the
mountains crumble flat,
Quick and dead shall be divided threefold; on this side,
and that,

The Companions of the right hand (ah! how joyful
they will be!)
The Companions of the left hand (oh! what misery to
see!)

Such, moreover, as of old time, loved the truth and
taught it well,
First in faith, they shall be foremost in reward: the
rest to Hell!

But those souls attaining Allah,—ah, the Gardens of
good cheer
Kept to lodge them! yea, besides the "Faithful,"
many will be there.

THE PEACE OF PARADISE.

Lightly lying on soft couches, beautiful with broidered gold,
Friends with friends, they shall be served by youths immortal, who will hold

Akwáb, abareek—cups and goblets—brimming with celestial wine—
Wine which hurts nor head nor stomach—this and fruits of Heaven which shine

Bright, desirable; and rich flesh of what birds they relish best;
Yea, and feasted, there shall soothe them damsels fairest, stateliest—

Damsels having eyes of wonder, large black eyes like hidden pearls,
Lulu-'l-maknún, Allah grants them, for sweet love, those matchless girls.

Never in that Garden hear they speech of folly, sin, or dread;
Only "Peace"—*As-Salâm* only—that one word for ever said,

"Peace! Peace! Peace!" and the Companions of the right hand (ah! those bowers!)
They shall roam in thornless lote-groves, under mawz-trees hung with flowers;

Shaded, fed by flowing waters; near to fruits which never cloy,
Hanging always ripe for plucking; and at hand the tender joy

Of those maids of Heaven, the Houris: lo! to them We gave a birth
Specially creating, lo! they are not as the wives of earth;

Ever virginal and stainless, how so often they embrace,
Always young and loved and loving these are; neither is there grace

Like the grace and bliss the Black-eyed keep for you in Paradise,
O Companions of the right hand! O ye others that were wise!*

*Giver of peace! when comes that day,
Set us within Thy sight, we pray.*

---

* Cf. Korân, lvi. chapter "Of the Inevitable."

7

Al-Maumin! "*Faithful,*" *fast, and just is He,*
And loveth such as live in verity.

IBN SÂWA, Lord of Bahrein, in the field
Captured a Sheikh, an Arab of the hills,
Sayid-bin-Tayf; and the king's oath was passed
That each tenth man of all the captives die
Together with their chieftains, for the war
Waxed fierce, and hearts of men were turned to flame.
So led they Sayid forth before the camp
At Azan; and a eunuch of the guard,
Savage and black, stood with his haick uprolled
Back to the armpit, and the scimetar's edge
Naked to strike.

    But suddenly the king
Inquired, "Art thou not he gave me to drink,
Hunting gazelles, before the war began?"
"Yea, I am he!" said Sayid.

      Quoth the king,
"Ask not thy life, but ask some other boon,
That I may pay my debt."

      Sayid replied,
"Death is not terrible to me who die
Red with this unbelieving blood of thine;
But there hath come a first-born in my tent;

Fain would I see my son's face for a day,
Before mine eyes are sealed. Lend me my life,
To hold as something borrowed from thy hand,
Which I will bring again."

"Ay!" laughed the king,
"If one should answer for it with his own.
Show me thy hostage!"

"Let me stand his bond,"
Spake one on whom the lot of mercy fell—
Ishâk of Tayf, a gallant youth and fair—
"I am his sister's son; bind ye my arms,
And set free Sayid, that he ride at speed,
And see his first-born's face, and come again."

So Sayid went free again, seeking his home.
But in the camp they mocked that faithful friend,
Saying, "Lo! as a fool thou diest now,
Staking thy life upon an Arab's word.
Why should he haste, to abide the bitter blade?
Will the scared jackal try the trap again;
The hawk once limed return unto the snare?
Cry to the desert-wind to turn and come,
But call not Sayid."

Ishâk only smiled,
And said, "He is a Muslim, he will come!"

The days passed, Sayid came not, and they led
The hostage forth, for Ishâk now must die;
But still he smiled, saying, "Till sunset's hour
Slay me not, for at sunset he will come."

So fell it, for the sun had touched the palms,
And that black swordsman stood again in act

THE VERITY OF SAYID.

To strike, when Sayid's white mare, galloping in,
Drew steaming breath before the royal tent;
And Sayid, leaping from the saddle, kissed
His kinsman's eyes, and gently spake to all,
"*Labbayki!* I am here."

      Then said the king,
"Never before was known a deed like this
That one should stake his life upon a word;
The other ride to death as to a bride.
Live, and be friends of Ibn Sâwa, but speak!
Whence learned ye these high lessons?"

       Ishâk spake,
"We are believers in the book which saith,
'Fulfil your covenants, if ye covenant;
For God is witness! break no word with men
Which God hath heard; and surely he hears all.'"*

That verse the king bade write in golden script
Over the palace gate; and he and his
Followed the Faith.

Ya! Allah-al-Maumin!
In truthfulness of act be our faith seen.

---

* Cf. Korân, xvi. chapter "Of the Bee."

8

Call Him Muhaimin, " Help in danger's hour,"
Protector of the true who trust His power.

THE spider and the dove!—what thing is weak
  If Allah makes it strong?
The spider and the dove!—if He protect,
  Fear thou not foeman's wrong.

From Mecca to Medina fled our Lord,
  The horsemen followed fast;
Into a cave to shun their murderous rage,
  Muhammad, weary, passed.

Quoth Abu Bekr, "If they see, we die!"
  Quoth Ebn Foheir, "Away!"
The guide Abdallah said, "The sand is deep,
  Those footmarks will betray."

Then spake our Lord, "We are not four, but Five;
  'He who protects' is here.
Come! Al-Muhaimin now will blind their eyes;
  Enter, and have no fear."

The band drew nigh; one of the Koreish cried,
  "Search ye out yonder cleft,
I see the print of sandalled feet which turn
  Thither, upon the left!"

But when they drew unto the cavern's mouth,
  Lo! at its entering-in,
A ring-necked desert dove sate on her eggs;
  The mate cooed soft within.

And right athwart the shadow of the cave
  A spider's web was spread;
The creature hung upon her net at watch;
  Unbroken was each thread.

"By Thammuz' blood," the unbelievers cried,
  "Our toil and time are lost;
Where doves hatch and the spider spins her snare
  No foot of man hath crossed!"

Thus did a desert bird and spider guard
  The blessed Prophet then;
For all things serve their Maker and their God
  Better than thankless men.

Allah-al-Muhaimin! shield and save
Us, for his sake within that cave.

9

Say Al-Hathim! He is the Mighty One!
Praise Him, and hear the great "Verse of the Throne."

"ALLAH! there is none other God but He,
   The Living God, the Self-subsistent One;
Weariness cometh not to Him, nor sleep;
   And whatso is belongs to Him alone
In heaven and earth; who is it intercedes
   With Him, save if He please? He is aware
What is before them and what after them,
   And they of all His knowledge nothing share
Save what He will vouchsafe. His throne's foundation
   Sits splendid, high above the earth and sky.
Which to sustain gives Him no meditation:
   Mightiest He is, Supreme in Majesty."

Ayatu-'l-Koorsîy! this we Muslims grave
On polished gem and painted architrave;
But thou, write its great letters on thy heart,
Lauding the Mighty One, whose work thou art.

10

The "All-Compelling!" golden is that verse,
Which doth His title—Al-Jabbár—rehearse.

SURA the nine and fiftieth: "Fear ye God,
O true believers! and let every soul
Heed what it doth to-day, because to-morrow
The same thing it shall find gone forward there
To meet and make and judge it. Fear ye God,
For He knows whatsoever deeds ye do.
Be not as those who have forgotten Him,
For they are those who have forgot themselves;
They are the evil-doers: not for such,
And for the heritors of Paradise,

Shall it be equal; Paradise is kept
For those thrice blessed who have ears to hear.

  Lo! had we sent "the Book" unto Our hills,
Our hills had bowed their crests in reverence,
And opened to the heart their breasts of rock
To take Heaven's message. Fear ye Him who knows
Present, and Past, and Future: fear ye Him
Who is the Only, Holy, Faithful Lord,
Glorious and good, compelling to His will
All things, for all things He hath made and rules.

So rule, Al-Jabbár; make our wills
Bend, though more stubborn than the hills.

11

Al-Mutakabbir! all the heavens declare
His majesty, Who makes them what they are.

AZAR, of Abraham the father, spake
Unto his son, "Come! and thine offerings make
Before the gods whose images divine
In Nimrûd's carved and painted temple shine.
Pay worship to the sun's great orb of gold;
Adore the queen-moon's silver state; behold
Otâred, Moshtari, Sohayl, in their might,
Those stars of glory, those high lords of light.
These have we wrought, as fitteth gods alone,
In bronze and ivory and chiselled stone.
Obey, as did thy sires, these powers of Heaven
Which rule the world, throned in the circles seven."

But Abraham said, "Did they not see the sun
Sink and grow darkened, when the days were done;
Did not the moon for them, too, wax and wane,
That they should pay her worship, false and vain?
Lo! all these stars have laws to rise and set—
Otâred, Moshtari, Sohayl—wilt thou yet
Bid me praise gods who humbly come and go,
Lights that a Greater Light hath kindled? No!
I dare not bow the knee to one of these;
My Lord is He who (past the sky man sees)
Waxeth and waneth not, Unchanged of all,
Him only 'God,' Him only 'Great,' I call."

Well spak'st thou, Friend of Allah! none
Is "great" except the Greatest One.

12

Praise the " Creator!" He who made us live,
Life everlasting unto us can give.

By the glorious Book We have sent! do they wonder a
    warner is come
Out from among themselves? do the misbelievers say
"This is a marvellous thing! what! when we are dead
    and dust
    To live! to arise! see now, this hope is a hope far
        away!"

But what the grave shall consume, and what of the
    man it shall leave,
    We know, for a roll is with Us where each soul's
        order is set.
Will they call the truth a lie when it cometh to them,
    and dwell
    Wrangling and foolish and fearful, confounding the
        matter? But yet

The heaven is above them to see how fair We have
    builded its arch,
    Painted it golden and blue, finished it perfect and
        clear;
And the earth how We spread it forth, and planted the
    mountains thereon;
    And made all the manifold trees and the beautiful
        blossoms appear.

Memorials are these to the wise, and a message to him
　　who repents;
　Moreover We drop from the clouds the blessing of
　　water, the rain,
Whereby the cool gardens do grow, and the palms
　　soaring up to the sky
　With their date-laden branches and boughs, one over
　　the other; and grain

To nourish the children of men. Lo! thus We have
　　quickened dead clay
　On the bosom of earth, and beneath her so, too, shall
　　a quickening be.

　　　.　　.　　.　　.　　.　　.　　.

What! deem they it wearied God to create?—that His
　　power was spent?
　They are fools, and they darken their eyes to that
　　which He willeth them see.

We have fashioned man, and we know the thoughts of
　　his innermost heart;
　We are closer to him than his blood, more near than
　　the vein of his throat;
At the right of ye all sits a watcher, a watcher sits at
　　your left;
　And whatso each speaketh or thinketh, those two
　　have known it and note.

Al-Khálik! Fashioner Divine!
Finish Thy work and make us Thine!

13

Al-Bâri! Moulder of each form and frame,
Pots praise the Potter, when we speak this name.

PRAISE be to God, the Designer, Builder of earth and
  of Heaven!
  Fashioned His Angels He hath, making them messengers still;
Two wings to some and four wings to some, and to
  some He hath given
  Six and eight silver wings, making what marvels
  He will.

Verily mighty is He, and what He bestoweth of
  blessing
  None can withhold; and none what He withholdeth
  can send;
Children of men! remember the mercies of Allah towards ye,
  Is there a Maker save this, is there another such
  Friend?

Nowhere another one, we see,
Wondrous "Artificer!" like Thee.

14

Al-Muzawwir! the "Fashioner!" say thus;
Still lauding Him who hath compounded us.

> WHEN the Lord would fashion men,
>   Spake He in the Angels' hearing,
> "Lo! Our will is there shall be
>   On the earth a creature bearing
> Rule and royalty. To-day
> We will shape a man from clay."
>
> Spake the Angels, "Wilt Thou make
>   Man who must forget his Maker,
> Working evil, shedding blood,
>   Of Thy precepts the forsaker?
> But Thou knowest all, and we
> Celebrate Thy majesty."
>
> Answered Allah, "Yea! I know
>   What ye know not of this making;
> Gabriel! Michael! Israfil!
>   Go down to the earth, and taking
> Seven clods of colors seven,
> Bring them unto Me in Heaven."
>
> Then those holy Angels three
>   Spread their pinions and descended;
> Seeking clods of diverse clay,
>   That all colors might be blended;

THE MAKING OF MAN.

Yellow, tawny, dun, black, brown,
White and red, as men are known.

But the earth spake, sore afraid,
  "Angels! of my substance take not;
Give me back my dust, and pray
  That the dread Creator make not
Man, for he will sin, and bring
Wrath on me and suffering."

Therefore empty-handed came
  Gabriel, Michael, Israfil,
Saying, "Lord! Thy earth imploreth
  Man may never on her dwell;
'He will sin and anger thee,
Give me back my clay!' cried she."

Spake the Lord to Azrael,
  "Go thou, who of wing art surest.
Tell my earth this shall be well;
  Bring those clods, which thou procurest
From her bosom, unto Me;
Shape them as I order thee."

Thus 'tis written how the Lord
  Fashioned Adam for His glory,
Whom the Angels worshipped,
  All save Iblîs; and this story
Teacheth wherefore Azrael saith,
"Come thou!" at man's hour of death.

Allah! when he doth call us, take!
We are such clay as Thou did'st make.

15

Al-Ghaffâr, the "Forgiver," praise thereby.
Thy Lord who is so full of clemency.

ONCE, it is written, Abraham, "God's Friend,"
Angered his Lord; for there had ridden in
Across the burning yellow desert-flats
An aged man, haggard with two days' drouth.
The water-skin swung from his saddle-fork
Wrinkled and dry; the dust clove to his lids,
And clogged his beard; his parched tongue and black lips
Moved to say, "Give me drink," yet uttered nought;
And that gaunt camel which he rode upon,
Sank to the earth at entering of the camp,
Too spent except to lay its neck along
The sand, and moan.　　　　To whom when they had given
The cool wet jar, asweat with diamond-drops
Of sparkling life, that way-worn Arab laved
The muzzle of his beast, and filled her mouth;
Then westward turned with blood-shot, worshipping eyes,
Pouring forth water to the setting orb:
Next, would have drunk, but Abraham saw, and said,
"Let not this unbeliever drink, who pours
God's gift of water forth unto the sun,
Which is but creature of the living Lord."

ABRAHAM'S OFFENCE.

But while the man still clutched the precious jar,
Striving to quaff, a form of grace drew nigh,
Beauteous, majestic. If he came afoot,
None knew, or if he glided from the sky.
With gentle air he filled a gourd and gave
The man to drink, and Abraham—in wrath
That one should disobey him in his tents—
Made to forbid; when full upon him smote
Eyes of divine light, eyes of high rebuke—
For this was Michael, Allah's messenger—
"Lo! God reproveth thee, thou Friend of God!
Forbiddest thou gift of the common stream
To this idolater, spent with the heat,
Who, in his utmost need, watered his beast,
And bowed the knee in reverence, ere he drank?
Allah hath borne with him these threescore years,
Bestowed upon him corn and wine, and made
His household fruitful and his herds increase;
And find'st thou not patience to pity him
Whom God hath pitied, waiting for the end,
Since none save He wotteth what end will come,
Or who shall find the light. Thou art rebuked!
Seek pardon! for thou hast much need to seek."

Thereat the Angel vanished, as he came;
But Abraham, with humbled countenance,
Kissed reverently the heathen's hand, and spake—
Leading him to the chief seat in the tent—
"God pardon me, as He doth pardon thee!"

Long-suffering Lord! ah, who should be
Forgiven, if Thou wert as we!

16

*Al-Kahhâr call Him—"Dominant," the King,
Who maketh, knoweth, ruleth everything.*

THE "Chapter of the Cattle:"* Heaven is whose,
And whose is earth? Say Allah's, That did choose
   On His own might to lay the law of mercy.
He, at the Resurrection, will not lose

One of His own. What falleth, night or day,
Falleth by His Almighty word alway.
   Wilt thou have any other Lord than Allah,
Who is not fed, but feedeth all flesh? Say!

For if He visit thee with woe, none makes
The woe to cease save He; and if He takes
   Pleasure to send thee pleasure, He is Master
Over all gifts; nor doth His thought forsake

The creatures of the field, nor fowls that fly;
They are "a people" also: "These, too, I
   Have set," the Lord saith, "in My book of record;
These shall be gathered to Me by and by."

With Him of all things secret are the keys;
None other hath them, but He hath; and sees
   Whatever is in land, or air, or water,
Each bloom that blows, each foam-bell on the seas.

---

* Cf. Korân, vi. chapter "Of the Cattle."

Nor is there any little hidden grain
Swelling beneath the sod, nor in the main
   Any small fish or shell, nor of the earth
Green things or dry things upon hill or plain,

But these are written in th' unerring Book:
And what ye did by day, and when ye took
   Your slumbers, and the last sleep; then to Him
Is your return, and the account's there!—look!

Al-Kahhár! All-embracing One!
Our trust is fixed on Thee alone.

17

*Praise "the Bestower:" unto all that live
He giveth, and He loveth those who give.*

THE Imâm Ali, Lion of the Faith,
Have ye not heard his giving? what he had
The poor had, for he held his gold and goods
As Allah's almoner. Ali it was
Who in the Mecca mosque at evening prayer—
Being entreated by some needy one—
Would not break off, yet would not let the man
Ask him in vain for what he asked of God,
Favor and aid; wherefore—amid the words—
He drew his emerald, carved with Allah's praise,
From his third finger, giving it; and prayed
With face unturned.

                If he had pieces ten,
He succored five score; if one dinar, then
Into ten dirhems he divided that,
And fed ten "people of the bench." Our Lord
(On whom be peace!) in all men's hearing said,
"This is the Prince of Givers!"

                        Once it fell,
Being sore hungered in his house, he cried,
"Fatmeh! thou daughter of the Prophet of God,
Find me to eat, if thou hast any food."

ALI AND THE ANGELS. 45

And Fatmeh said, "Father of Hassan! here
Not a dry date is left—not one—I swear
By Him besides Whom is none other God;
But in the corner of the tomb I laid
Six silver akchas: take them, if thou wilt,
And buy thee in the market food, and bring
Fruits for our boys, Hassan and Hussain." Thus
Ali departed. On his way he spied
Two Mussulmans, of whom one rudely haled
The other, crying, "Pay thy debt, or come
Unto the prison where the smiter waits."
And he who owed had nought, and wept amain,
Sighing, "Alas the day!" But Ali asked,
"What is thy debt, my brother?" Then he moaned,
"Six akchas, for the lack of which the chains
Must load me." "Nay!" spake Ali, "they are here;
Take them and pay the man, and go in peace."
So went that debtor free, but Ali came
Empty in hand and belly home again
Unto his door, where Fatmeh and the sons,
Hassan and Hussain, seeing him approach,
Ran joyous forth, crying, "He bringeth us
Dates now, and honey, and new camels' milk;
Soon shall we feast." But when they saw his cloth
Hang void, and troubled eyes, and heard him say,
"Upon my road I met a poorer man
Who, for six akchas, should have borne the chains;
To him I gave them, and I bring ye nought,"
Then the lads wept; but Fatmeh smiled and spake:
"Well hast thou done, O servant of the Lord!
Weep not, ye sons of Ali, though we fast;
Who feedeth Allah's children, feasts His own:
He, the 'Bestower,' will provide for us."

But Ali turned, heart-sore because the boys
Lacked meat, and Fatmeh's lovely eyes were sunk
Hollow with hunger. "I will go," thought he,
"Unto the blessed Prophet, for, if one
Be burdened with a thousand woes, his word
Dismisses them and makes the sorrow joy."
So bent he mournful steps thither, to tell
The Lord Muhammad of this strait, when—lo!
An Arab in mid path encountered him,
Of noble bearing, with a chieftain's mien,
Leading a riding-camel by her string,
Black, with full teeth, the best beast ever foaled.
"Buy Wurdah!—buy my desert rose," quoth he;
"One hundred akchas make her thine, so thou
Shalt own the best in Hedjaz, or at choice
Sell her for double money." Ali said,
"The beast is excellent! fain would I buy,
But have not in my scrip thy price." "Go to,"
The Sheikh replied; "take her and bring thy gold,
When Allah pleaseth, to the western gate;
I will await thee."

Ali nodded; took
The nose-string, turning to the left to seek
The camel-merchants that should buy the beast;
Whom at the very entry of the Khan
Another Arab in the desert garb,
Lordly and gracious like his fellow, met,
And quick saluted, saying, "Peace with thee!
God send thee favor! wilt thou sell me now
Thy riding-camel with the great stag-eyes?
Here be three hundred akchas counted down,
Silver and gold, good money! Such an one

I sought, but found not, till I saw thee here."
"If thou wilt buy," quoth Ali, "be it so!"
And thereupon that Bedawee counted out
Dinars and dirhems—little suns and moons
Of glittering gold and silver—in his cloth,
And took the beast; but Ali, with one piece
Bought food and fruits, and, hastening home again,
Heard his lads laugh with joy to see the store
Poured forth;—white cakes and dates and amber grapes—
And smiled himself to mark Fatmeh's soft eyes
Gladden; then, having eaten, blessed the Lord,
Giver of gifts, "Bestower."

So, once more
Made he to go unto the western gate
To pay his seller; but upon the street
The Prophet met him. Lightly smiled our Lord,
(On whom be comfort!) lightly questioned he,
Saying, "O Ali! who was he did sell
Thy riding-camel, and to whom didst thou
Sell her again?" Quoth Ali, "Only God
Knoweth, except thou knowest!" Spake our Lord,
"Yea, but I know! that was great Gabriel,
Chief messenger of Heaven, from whom thou bought'st;
And he to whom thou sold'st was Israfil,
His heavenly fellow; and that beast did come
Forth from the pleasure-fields of Paradise,
And thither back is gone; for—look! my son,
Allah hath recompensed thee fifty times
The goodly deed thou didst, giving thine all
To free the weeping debtor. Oh, He sees
And measures and bestows; but what is kept,

Beyond gifts here, for kindly hearts that love,
God only wotteth, and the Eternal Peace."

———

Bestower! grant us grace to see
Our gain is what we lose for Thee.

18

Al-Razzâk! the " Provider !" thus again
Praise Him who, having formed thee, doth sustain.

By the high dawn,
When the light of the sun is strong!
By the thick night,
When the darkness is deep and long!
He hath not forsook thee, nor hated!
By his mercies, I say,
The life which will come shall be better
Than the life of to-day.

In the latter days
The Lord thy "Provider" shall give;
When thou knowest His gift
Thou wilt not ask rather to live;
Look back! thou wert friendless and frameless,
He made thee from nought;
Look back! thou wert blinded and wandering,
To the light thou art brought!
Consider! shall Allah forego thee
Since thus He hath wrought? *

The favor of thy Lord perpend,
And praise His mercies without end.

---

* Cf. Korân, xciii. chapter "Of the Forenoon."

19

*Al-Fattá'h! praise the "Opener!" and recite
The marvels of that "Journey of the Night."**

Our Lord Muhammad lay upon the hill
   Safâ, whereby the holy city stands,
     Asleep, wrapped in a robe of camels' wool.
Dark was the night—that Night of grace—and still;
   When all the seven spheres, by God's commands,
     Opened unto him, splendid and wonderful!

For Gabriel, softly lighting, touched his side,
   Saying, "Rise, thou enwrapped one! come and see
     The things which be beyond. Lo! I have brought
Borak, the horse of swiftness; mount and ride!"
   Milk-white that steed was, with embroidery
     Of pearls and emeralds in his long hair wrought.

Hooved like a mule he was, with a man's face;
   His eyes gleamed from his forelock, each a star
     Of lucent hyacinth; the saddle-cloth
Was woven gold, which priceless work did grace!
   The lightning goeth not so fast or far
     As those broad pinions which he fluttered forth.

One heel he smote on Safâ, and one heel
   On Sinai—where the dint is to this day.

---

* Cf. Korân, xvii. chapter "Of the Night Journey."

MUHAMMAD'S JOURNEY TO HEAVEN. 51

Next at Jerusalem he neighed. Our Lord,
Descending with th' Archangel there, did kneel
 Making the midnight prayer; afterwards they
  Tethered him to the Temple by a cord.

"Ascend!" spake Gabriel; and behold! there fell
 Out of the sky a ladder bright and great,
  Whereby, with easy steps, on radiant stairs,
They mounted—past our earth and heaven and hell—
 To the first sphere, where Adam kept the gate,
  Which was of vaporous gold and silvery squares

Here thronged the lesser Angels: some took charge
 To fill the clouds with rain and speed them round,
  And some to tend live creatures; for what's born
Hath guardians there in its own shape: a large
 Beauteous white cock crowed matins, at the sound
  Cocks in a thousand planets hailed the morn.

Unto the second sphere by that white slope
 Ascended they, whereof Noah held the key;
  And two-fold was the throng of Angels here;
But all so dazzling glowed its fretted cope,
 Burning with beams, Muhammad could not see
  What manner of celestial folk were there.

The third sphere lay a thousand years beyond
 If thou should'st journey as the sun-ray doth,
  But in one *Fátihah* clomb they thitherward.
David and Solomon in union fond
 Ruled at the entrance, keeping Sabaoth
  Of ceaseless joy. The void was paven hard

With paven work of rubies—if there be
 Jewels on earth to liken unto them

Which had such color as no goldsmith knows—
And here a vast Archangel they did see,
  "Faithful of God" his name, whose diadem
    Was set with peopled stars; wherefrom arose

Lauds to the glory of God, filling the blue
  With lovely music, as rose-gardens fill
    A land with essences; and young stars, shaking
Tresses of lovely light, gathered and grew
  Under his mighty plumes, departing still
    Like ships with crews and treasure, voyage-making.

So came they to the fourth sphere, where there sate
  Enoch, who never tasted death; and there
    Behind its portal awful Azrael writes;
The shadow of his brows compassionate
  Made night across all worlds; our Lord felt fear,
    Marking the stern eyes and the hand which smites.

For always on a scroll he sets the names
  Of new-born beings, and from off the scroll
    He blotteth who must die; and holy tears
Roll down his cheeks, recording all our shames
  And sins and penalties; while of each soul
    Monker and Nakir reckon the arrears.

Next, at the fifth sphere's entry, they were 'ware
  Of a door built in sapphire, having graven
    Letters of flashing fire, the faith unfolding,
"THERE IS NO GOD SAVE GOD." Aaron sate there
  Guarding the "region of the wrath of Heaven;"
    And Israfil behind, his trumpet holding,

His trumpet holding—which shall wake the dead
  And slay the living—all his cheek puffed out,

MUHAMMAD'S JOURNEY TO HEAVEN. 53

    Bursting to blow; for none knows Allah's time,
Nor when the word of judgment shall be said:
    And darts, and chains of flame, lay all around,
    Terrible tortures for th' ungodly's crime.

When to the sixth sphere passed they, Moses sped
    Its bars of chrysoprase, and kissed our Lord,
    And spake full sweet, "Prophet of Allah! thou
More souls of Ismael's tribes to truth hast led,
    Than I of Isaak's." Here the crystal sword
    Of Michael gave the light they journeyed through.

But at the seventh sphere that light which shone
    Hath not an earthly name, nor any voice
    Can tell its splendor, nay, nor any ear
Learn, if it listened; only he alone
    Who saw it, knows how there th' elect rejoice,
    Isa, and Ibrahim, and the souls most dear.

And he, the glorious regent of that sphere,
    Had seventy thousand heads; and every head
    As many countenances; and each face
As many mouths; and in each mouth there were
    Tongues seventy thousand, whereof each tongue said,
    Ever and ever, "Praise to Allah! praise!"

Here, at the bound, is fixed that lotus-tree.
    SEDRA, which none among the Angels pass;
    And not great Gabriel's self might farther wend:
Yet, led by presences too bright to see,
    Too high to name, on paths like purple glass
    Our Lord Muhammad journeyed to the end.

Alone! alone! through hosts of Cherubim
    Crowding the infinite void with whispering vans,

From splendor unto splendor still he sped;
Across the "Lake of Gloom" they ferried him,
  And then the "Sea of Glory:" mortal man's
    Heart cannot hold the wonders witnessĕd.

So to the "Region of the Veils" he came,
  Which shut all times off from eternity,
    The bars of being where thought cannot reach:
Ten thousand thousand are they, walls of flame
  Lambent with loveliness and mystery,
    Ramparts of utmost heaven, having no breach.

Then he SAW GOD! our Prophet saw THE THRONE!—
  O Allah! let these weak words be forgiven!—
    Thou, the Supreme, "the Opener," spake at last;
The Throne! the Throne! he saw;—our Lord alone!
  Saw it and heard!—but the verse falls from heaven
    Like a poised eagle, whom the lightnings blast.

    .   .   .   .

And Gabriel waiting by the tree he found;
  And Borak, tethered to the Temple porch;
    He loosed the horse, and 'twixt its wings ascended.
One hoof it smote on Zion's hallowed ground,
  One upon Sinai; and the day-star's torch
    Was not yet fading when the journey ended.

Al-Fáttá'h! "*Opener!*" *we say*
Thy name, and worship Thee alway.

20

Al-'Alim! the "All-Knower!" by this word
Praise Him Who sees th' unseen, and hears th' unheard.

IF ye keep hidden your mind, if ye declare it aloud,
  Equally God hath perceived, equally known is each thought:
If on your housetops ye sin, if in dark chambers ye shroud,
  Equally God hath beheld, equally judgment is wrought.

He, without listing, doth know how many breathings ye make;
  Numbereth the hairs of your heads, wotteth the beats of your blood;
Heareth the feet of the ant when she wanders by night in the brake;
  Counteth the eggs of the snake and the cubs of the wolf in the wood.

Mute the Moakkibât* sit this side and that side of men,
  One on the right noting good, and one on the left noting ill;
Each hath those Angels beside him who write with invisible pen
  Whatso he doeth, or sayeth, or thinketh, recording it still.

---

* These are the "Successors," or Angels of Record, who relieve each other in the duty of registering human actions, etc.

Vast is the mercy of God, and when a man doeth aright,
  Glad is the right-hand Angel, and setteth it quick on
    the roll;
Ten times he setteth it down in letters of heavenly
    light,
  For one good deed ten deeds, and a hundred for ten
    on the scroll.

But when one doeth amiss the right-hand Angel doth
    lay
  His palm on the left-hand Angel and whispers, "Forbear thy pen!
Peradventure in seven hours the man may repent him
    and pray;
  At the end of the seventh hour, if it must be, witness
    it then."*

Al-'Alim! Thou Who knowest all,
With hearts unveiled on Thee we call.

---

* Cf. Korân, xiii. chapter "Of thunder."

21

Yakbuzu wa Yabsutu! heaven and hell
He closeth and uncloseth—and doth well! *

IN gold and silk and robes of pride
An evil-hearted monarch died;
Pampered and arrogant his soul
Quitted the grave. His eyes did roll
Hither and thither, deeming some
In that new world should surely come
To lead his spirit to a seat
Of state, for kingly merit meet.
What saw he? 'twas a hag so foul
There is no Afrit, Djin, or Ghoul
With countenance as vile, or mien
As fearful, and such terrors seen
In the fierce voice and hideous air,
Blood-dripping hands and matted hair.
"Allah have mercy!" cried the king,
"Whence and what art thou, hateful thing?"
"Dost thou not know—who gav'st me birth?"
Replied the form; "thy sins on earth
In me embodied thus behold.
I am thy wicked work! unfold
Thine arms and clasp me, for we two
In hell must live thy sentence through."

---

* Cf. Korân, ii. chapter "Of the Cow."

Then with a bitter cry, 'tis writ,
The king's soul passed unto the pit.

———

Al-Kabiz! so He bars the gate
Against the unregenerate.

22

Yet He who shuts the gate, just wrath to wreak,
Unbars it, full of mercy, to the meek.

THERE died upon the Miraj night,
A man of Mecca, Amru height;
Faithful and true, patient and pure,
Had been his years; he did endure
In war five spear-wounds, and in peace
Long journeying for his tribe's increase;
And ever of his gains he gave
Unto poor brethren—kind as brave:
But these forsook, and age and toil
Drained the strong heart as flames drink oil;
Till, lone and friendless, gray and spent—
A thorn-tree's shadow for his tent,
And desert sand for dying-bed—
Amru the camel-man lay dead.

What is it that the 'Hadîth saith?
Even while the true eyes glazed in death,
And the warm heart wearied, and beat
The last drum of its long defeat,
An Angel, lighting on the sand,
Took Amru's spirit by the hand,
And gently spake, "Dear brother, come!
A sore road thou didst journey home;

But life's dry desert thou hast passed,
And Zem-Zem sparkles nigh at last."
Then with swift flight those twain did rise
Unto the gates of Paradise,
Which opened, and the Angel gave
A golden granate, saying, "Cleave
This fruit, my brother!" But its scent
So heavenly seemed, and so intent,
So rapt was Amru, to behold
The great fruit's rind of blushing gold
And emerald leaves—he dared not touch,
Murmuring, "O Mâlik! 'tis too much
That I am here, with eyes so dim,
And grace all fled." Then bade they him
Gaze in the stream which glided stilly,
'Mid water-roses and white lily,
Under those lawns and smiling skies
That make delight in Paradise;
When, lo! the presence imaged there
Was of such comeliness, no peer
Among those glorious Angels stood
To Amru, mirrored in the flood.

"I! is it I?" he cried in gladness,
"Am I so changed from toil and sadness?"
"This was thy hidden self," replied
The Angels. "So shalt thou abide
By our bright river evermore;
And in that fair fruit's secret core—
Which on the Tree of Life hath grown—
Another marvel shall be shown.
Ah, happy Amru! cleave!" He clove:—
Sweet miracle of bliss and love!

GOOD DEEDS.

Forth from the pomegranate there grew,
As from its bud a rose breaks through,
A lovely, stately, lustrous maid,
Whose black orbs long silk lashes shade,
Whose beauty was so rich to see
No verse can tell it worthily;
Nor is there found in any place
One like her for the perfect grace
Of soft arms wreathed and ripe lips moving
In accents musical and loving;
For thus she spake: "Peace be to thee,
My Amru!" Then, with quick cry, he:
"Who art thou, blessed one? what name
Wearest thou? teach my tongue to frame
This worship of my heart." Said she,
"Thy good deeds gave me being: see,
If in my beauty thou hast pleasure,
How the Most High doth truly treasure
Joy for his servants. Murzieh I—
She that doth love and satisfy—
And I am made by Allah's hand
Of ambergris and musk, to stand
Beside thee, soothing thee, and tending
In comfort and in peace unending."

So hand in hand, 'tis writ, they went
To those bright bowers of high content.

Al-Bâsit! thus He opens wide
His mercies to the justified.

23

Al-Khâfiz! the "Abaser!" praise hereby
Him Who doth mock at earthly majesty.

HEARD ye of Nimrûd? Cities fell before him;
　Shinar, from Accad to the Indian Sea,
His garden was; as God, men did adore him;
　Queens were his slaves, and kings his vassalry.

Eminent on his car of carven brass,
　Through foeman's blood nave-deep he drave his wheel;
And not a lion in the river-grass
　Could keep its shaggy fell from Nimrûd's steel.

But he scorned Allah, schemed a tower to invade Him;
　Dreamed to scale Heaven, and measure might with God;
Heaped high the foolish clay wherefrom We made him,
　And built thereon his seven-fold house of the clod.

Therefore, the least Our messengers among,
　We sent;—a gray gnat dancing in the reeds:
Into his ear she crept, buzzing,—and stung.
　So perished mighty Nimrûd and his deeds.

O Thou Abaser of all pride!
Mighty Thou art, and none beside.

24

Ar-Râfi! the "Exalter!" laud Him so
Who loves the humble and lifts up the low.

WHOM hath He chosen for His priests and preachers,
   Lords who were eminent, or men of might?
Nay, but consider how He seeks His teachers,
   Hidden, like rubies unaware of light.

Ur of the Chaldees! what chance to discover
   Th' elect of Heaven in Azar's leathern tent?
But Allah saw his child, and friend, and lover,
   And Abraham was born, and sealed, and sent.

The babe committed to th' Egyptian water!
   Knew any that the tide of Nilus laved
The hope of Israel there? yet Pharaoh's daughter
   Found the frail ark, and so was Moses saved.

Low lies the Syrian town behind the mountain
   Where Mary, meek and spotless, knelt that morn,
And saw the splendid Angel by the fountain,
   And heard his voice, "Lord Isa shall be born!"

Nay, and Muhammad (blessed may he be!),
   Abdallah's and Amînah's holy son,
Whom black Halîmah nursed, the Bedawee,
   Where lived a lonelier or a humbler one?

Think how *he* led the camels of Khadîjah,
  Poor, but illumined by the light of Heaven;
Mightier than Noah, or Enoch, or Elijah,
  Our holy Prophet to Arabia given.

Man knew him not, wrapped in his cloth, and weeping
  Lonely on Hirâ all that wondrous night;
But Allah for his own our Lord was keeping:—
  "Rise, thou enwrapped one!" Gabriel spake, "and write."

*Save God there is none high at all,
Nor any low whom He doth call.*

25

*Al-Muhizz! by this title celebrate
The "Honorer" Whose favor maketh great.*

SAY "God," say "Lord of all!
Kingdoms and kings Thou makest and unmakest,
This one Thou takest, that one Thou forsakest;
    Alike are great and small;
    Into Thy hand they fall."

"In Thy dread hand they rest;
Their nights and days, their waking and their sleeping,
Their birth, and life, and death lie in Thy keeping;
    'Be thus' to each Thou say'st,
    And thus to be is best,

"Though it seem good or ill.
Islâm!—to Thee our souls we do resign,
Turning our faces to the blessed shrine;
    Seeking no honor still
    Save from Thy will."*

*Al-Muhizz! only this we pray
To learn Thy will and to obey.*

---

* Cf. Korân, iii. chapter "Of Imran's Family."

26

*O, Al-Muzîl! what if it be Thy will,
Having made man, to lead him into ill?*

SAITH the Perspicuous Book: "All things which be are
 of God;
 Neither, except by His word, falleth a leaf to the
 ground;
If He will open He openeth, and whom He hath blinded
 He blindeth,
 Leading, misleading; to none liable, blamable,
 bound."*

Saith the Perspicuous Book: "Tied on the neck of a
 man
 Hangeth the scroll of his fate, not a line to be gain-
 said or grudged;
When the trumpet of Israfil thunders, the Angels will
 show it and say,
 Read there what thine own deeds have written;
 thyself by thyself shall be judged." †

Wilt thou be wiser than God Who knoweth beginning
 and end?
Wilt thou be juster than He whose balance is turned
 by a sigh?

---

* Cf. Korân, iii. chapter " Of Imran's Family."
† Cf. Korân, xvii. chapter " Of the Night Journey."

He sayeth, "It shall not be equal for the doers of right and of wrong."

"It shall not be equal," He sayeth, "for them that accept and deny." *

Al-Muzîl! lead us not astray!
Teach us to find the perfect way.

---

* Cf. Korân, *eodem loco.*

27

*As-Samí'h! O Thou Hearer! none can be
So far, his crying doth not come to Thee.*

WRITES in his Mesnevî, Jelâlu-'d-deen:
There came a man of Yaman, poor and old,
To Mecca, making pilgrimage; untaught,
A shepherd of the hills. Humble he trod
The six mikât, the stages of the Hadj;
Humbly indued the ihrâm, garb of faith
Which hath no seam; made due ablutions, kissed
The black stone; then three times with hastening feet
Circled the Kaabah, and four times paced
With slackened gate the tawâf, as is due,
(For such observances the Mollah taught).
But, when he bowed before the Holy Place,
Thus brake his soul from him, knowing no prayer,
Full of God's love, though ignorant of God:
"O Master! O my Sheikh! where tarriest Thou?
Show me Thy face that I may worship Thee,
May toil Thy servant, which I am in heart:
Ah! let me sew Thy shoes, anoint Thine hair,
Wash Thy soiled robes, and serve Thee daily up
My she-goats' freshest milk—I love thee so!
Where hidest Thou, that I may kiss Thine hand,
Chafe Thy dear feet, and ere Thou takest rest—
In the gold sky, beside Thy sun, belike,

A SHEPHERD'S PRAYER.

Among the soft-spread fleeces of Thy clouds—
Sweep out Thy chamber, O my joy, my King!"

Which hearing, they who kept the shrine, incensed,
Had haled him to the gateway, crying, "Dog!
What blasphemy is this thou utterest,
Saying such things of Him That hath no needs
Of nourishment, nor clothing, nor repose,
Nor hands, nor feet, nor any form or frame;
That thou, base keeper of the silly herd,
Shouldst proffer service to the All-Powerful?
Meet were it that we stoned thee dead with stones,
Who art accursed and injurious.
Beyond! these holy walls are not for thee."

So, sore abashed, that shepherd made to go,
Silent and weeping; but our Prophet marked,
And with mild eyes smiled on the man; then spake
To those that drave him forth: "Ye, when ye pray
Outside this holy place, in distant lands,
Whither turn ye your faces?" Each one said,
"Unto the Kaabah." "And when ye pray,
Within the blessed precincts, pilgrims here,
Which way lies Mecca?" "All is sacred here,"
They answered, "and it matters nought which way."
"Lo! now ye reason well," replied our Lord;
"Inside the Kaabah it matters nought
Whither men turn; and in the secret place
Of perfect love for God, words are as breath
And will is all. This simple shepherd's prayer
Came unto Allah's ears clearer than yours,
Nathless his ignorance, because his heart—
Not tongue, not understanding—uttered it.

Make room for God's poor lover nighest me;
Good fellowship hath any man with him
To whom Heaven's ear as quick inclines itself
As doth a mother's when her babe lisps love."

Then were they sore ashamèd in that hour.

Hearer of hearts! As-Samí'h! so
Our love inspire, and Thine bestow.

28

*Al-Bazîr! O Thou Seer! great and small
Live in Thy vision, which embraceth all.*

WERE it one wasted seed of water-grass,
Blown by the wind, or buried in the sand,
He seeth and ordaineth if it live;
Were it a wild bee questing honey-buds,
He seeth if she find, and how she comes
On busy winglets to her hollow tree.
The seeing of His eyes should not be told,
Though all the reeds in all the earth were cut
To writing-sticks, and all the seven seas
Were seven times multiplied, flowing with ink,
And seventy angels wrote. He beholds all
Which was, or is, or will be: yea, with Him
Is present vision of five secret things:
The day of Judgment; and the times of rain;
The child hid in the womb—is quickenring,
And whether male or female;—what will fall
To-morrow (as ye know what did befall
Yesterday); and where every man shall die.*

"Where every man shall die." Al Beidhâwi
Presenteth how there sate with Solomon
A prince of India, and there passed them by
Azrael, Angel of Death, on shadowy plumes;

---

* Cf. Korân, xxxi. chapter "Of Lokman."

With great eyes gazing earnestly, as one
Who wonders, gazing. And, because the prince
Sate with the king, he saw what the king saw,
The Djins and Angels, and saw Azrael
Fixing on him those awful searching eyes.
"What name, I pray thee, wears yon messenger?"
So asked he of the king; and Solomon
Made answer, "It is Azrael, who calls
The souls of men." "He seemed," whispered the prince,
"To have an errand unto me;—bid now
That one among thy demon ministers
Waft me, upon the swiftest wing that beats,
To India, for I fear him." Solomon
Issued command, and a swift Djin sprang forth
Bearing the prince aloft, so that he came
To Coromandel, ere the fruit—which fell
Out of the fig—had touched the marble floor.

Thereupon Azrael said to Solomon,
"I looked thus earnestly upon the man
In wonder, for my Lord spake, 'Take his soul
In India;' yet behold he talked with thee
Here in Judæa! Now, see! he hath gone
There where it was commanded he should die."

Then followed Azrael. In that hour the prince
Died of a hurt, sitting in India.

With Thee, Lord, be the time and place,
So that we die in Thy dear grace.

29

*Al-Hâkim! think upon the Day of Doom,
And fear "the Judge" before Whom all must come.*

WHEN the sun is withered up,
And the stars from Heaven roll;
When the mountains quake,
And ye let stray your she-camels, gone ten months in foal;
When wild beasts flock
With the people and the cattle
In terror, in amazement,
And the seas boil and rattle;
And the dead souls
For their bodies seek;
And the child vilely slain
Is bid to speak,
Being asked, "Who killed thee, little maid?
Tell us his name!"
While the books are unsealed,
And crimson flame
Flayeth the skin of the skies,
And Hell breaks ablaze;
And Paradise
Opens her beautiful gates to the gaze;—
Then shall each soul
Know the issues of the whole,
And the balance of its scroll.*

---

* Cf. Korân, lxxxi. chapter "Of the Folding Up."

Shall We swear by the stars
Which fade away?
By the Night drowned in darkness,
By the dead Day?
We swear not! a true thing is this;
It standeth sure,
He saw it and he heard, and Our word
Will endure!

. . . .

When the sky cleaves asunder,
And the stars
Are scattered; and in thunder
All the bars
Of the seas burst, and all the graves are emptied
Like chests upturned,
Each soul shall see her doings, done and undone,
And what is earned.
The smiting, the smiting
Of that Day!
The horror, the splendor,
Who shall say? *
The Day when none shall answer for his brother;
The Day which is with God, and with none other.

---

*Al-Hâkim! Judge! Save by Thy power,
Who might abide that awful hour?*

---

* Cf. Korân, lxxxii. chapter " Of Cleaving Asunder."

30

Al-Hâdil! O " Just Lord!" we magnify
Thy righteous Law, which shall the whole world try.

GOD will roll up, when this world's end approacheth,
  The broad blue spangled hangings of the sky,
Even as As-Sigill * rolleth up his record,
  And seals and binds it when a man doth die.

Then the false worshippers, and what they follow,
  Will to the pit, like "stones of hell," descend;
But true believers shall hear Angels saying,
  "This is your day; be joyous without end." †

In that hour dust shall lie on many faces,
  And may faces shall be glad and bright; ‡
Ye who believe, trust and be patient always,
  Until God judges, for He judges right. §

Give us to pass before Thy throne
Among the number of Thine own!

---

* A name of the Angel of Registration.
† Cf. Korân, xxi. chapter "Of the Prophets."
‡ Cf. Korân, lxxx. chapter "Of the Frown."
§ Cf. Korân, x. chapter "Of Jonas."

31

Dread is His wrath, but boundless is His grace,
Al-Latîf! Lord! show us Thy "favoring" face!

> Most quick to pardon sins is He:
>   Who unto God draws near
> One forward step, God taketh three
>   To meet, and quit his fear.

> If ye will have of this world's show,
>   God grants, while Angels weep;
> If ye for Paradise will sow,
>   Right noble crops ye reap.*

Ah, Gracious One, we toil to reap:
The soil is hard, the way is steep!

---

* Cf. Korân, xlii. chapter "Of Counsel."

32

*Al-Khabîr! Thou Who art "aware" of all,
By this name also for Thy grace we call.*

ONE morning in Medina walked our Lord
Among the tombs: glad was the dawn, and broad
On headstones and on footstones sunshine lay;
Earth seemed so fair, 'twas hard to be away.
" O people of the graves!" Muhammad said,
" Peace be with you! Your caravan of dead
Hath passed the defile, and we living ones
Forget what men ye were, of whom the sons,
And what your merchandise and where ye went;
But Allah knows these things! Be ye content
Since Allah is 'aware.' Ah! God forgive
Those that are dead, and us who briefly live."

---

*Yea! pardon, Lord, since Thou dost know
To-morrow, now, and long ago.*

33

Al-Hâlim! "*Clement*" *is our Lord above;*
Magnify Allah by this name of love.

YE know the ant that creeps upon the fig,
   The *dharra*, made so small,
Until she moveth in the purple seeds
   She is not seen at all.

If, on the judgment-day, holding the scales—
   When all the trial's done—
The Angel of the Balance crieth, "Lord!
   The good deeds of this one

Outweigh his evil deeds, justly assessed,
   By half one *dharra's* weight;"
Allah will say, "Multiply good to him,
   And open Heaven's gate!"

Not if thy work be worth a date-stone's skin
   Shall it be overpast;
Thus it is written in the Sacred Book,*
   Thus will it be at last.

Faithful and just, Al-Hâlim! we
Take refuge in Thy clemency.

---

* Cf. Korân, iv. chapter "Of Women."

34

Al-'Aziz! " Strong and Sovereign" God, Thy hand
Is over all Thy works, holding command.

MAKER of all ye truly call the Strong and Sovereign
   One,
Yet have ye read that verse which saith whereto His
   work was done?
Open "the Book," and, heedful, look what weighty
   words are given
(The Chapter of Al-Akhâf) concerning Earth and
   Heaven.

"The Heavens and earth," Al-Akhâf saith, "and
   whatso is between,
Think ye that We made these to be, and then—not to
   have been?
Think ye We fashioned them in jest, without their
   times, and plan,
And purpose? Nay! accurst are they who judge of
   God by man."*

O Higher, Wiser, than we know,
Let not Thy creatures judge Thee so.

---

* Cf. Korân, xlvi. chapter "Of Al-Akhâf."

35

He is the "Pardoner," and his Scripture hath—
"Paradise is for them that check their wrath,
And pardon sins; so Allah doth with souls;
He loveth best him who himself controls." *

KNOW ye of Hassan's slave? Hassan the son
Of Ali. In the camp at Ras-al-hadd
He made a banquet unto sheikhs and lords,
Rich dressed and joyous; and a slave bore round,
Smoking with new-cooked pillaw, Badhan's dish
Carved from rock-crystal, with the feet in gold,
And garnets round the rim; but the boy slipped
Against the tent-rope, and the precious dish
Broke into shards of beauty on the board,
Scalding the son of Ali. One guest cried,
"Dog! wert thou mine, for this thing thou shouldst
  howl!"
Another, "Wretch! thou meritest to die."
And yet another, "Hassan! give me leave
To smite away this swine's head with my sword!"
Even Hassan's self was moved; but the boy fell
Face to the earth and cried, "My lord! 'tis writ,
'*Paradise is for them that check their wrath.*'"
"'Tis writ so," Hassan said; "I am not wroth."
"My lord!" the boy sobbed on, "also 'tis writ,
'*Pardon the trespasser.*'" Hassan replied,

---

* Cf. Korân, iii. chapter "Of Imran's Family."

"'Tis written—I remember—I forgive."
" Now is the blessing of the Most High God
On thee, dear master!" cried the happy slave,
" For He—'tis writ—' *loves the beneficent.*' "
" Yea! I remember, and I thank thee, slave,"
Quoth Hassan;—" better is one noble verse
Fetched from ' the Book,' than gold and crystal brought
From Yaman's hills. Lords! he hath marred the dish,
But mended fault with wisdom. See, my slave!
I give thee freedom, and this purse to buy
The robe and turban of a Muslim freed."

Al-Ghâfir! pardon us, as we
Forgive a brother's injury.

36

*"Grateful"—Ash-Shâkir—is He; praise Him so
Who thanketh men for that He did bestow.*

So much hast thou of thy hoard
As thou gavest to thy Lord;
Only this will bring thee in
Usance rich and free from sin:
Send thy silver on before,
Lending to His sick and poor.
Every dirhem dropped in alms
Touches Allah's open palms,
Ere it fall into the hands
Of thy brother. Allah stands
Begging of thee, when thy brother
Asketh help. Ah! if another
Proffered thee, for meat and drink,
Food upon Al-Kâuthar's brink,*
Shining Kâuthar which doth flow
Sweet as honey, cool as snow,
White as milk, and smooth as cream,
Underneath its banks, which gleam—
Green and golden chrysolite,
In the Gardens of delight,
Whence who drinks never again
Tasteth sorrow, age, or pain—

---

* Cf. Korân, cviii.

SURA "OF AL-KAUTHAR."

Who would not make merchandise,
Buying bliss in Paradise,
Laying up his treasure where
Stores are safe and profits clear?
But ye lend at lower cost,
Whilst Ash-Shâkir offers most,
Good returning seven times seven,
Paying gifts of earth with Heaven.

Allah, Who dost reward so well,
What maketh man in sin to dwell?

37

Al-'Hali! O believers, magnify
By this great name, Allah, our Lord " Most High."

He willed, and Heaven's blue arch vaulted the air;
 "Be!" said He—Earth!* and the round earth was made;
See! at the hour of late and early prayer
 The very shadows worship Him, low laid.

Most High! the lengthening shadows teach
Morning and evening prayer to each.

---

* Cf. Korân, xvi. chapter "Of the Bee."

38

Praise Him, Al-Kabír, seated on "the Throne,"
The "Very Great," the High-exalted One.

SEVEN Heavens Allah made:
First "Paradise," the *Jennat-al-Firdaus;*
The next, *Al Huld*, "Gate of Eternity;"
The third, *Dar-as-Salâm*, the "Peaceful House;"
The fourth, *Dar-al-Kurâr*, "Felicity;"
The fifth was *Aidenn*, "Home of Golden Light;"
The sixth, *Al Na'hîm*, "Garden of Delight;"
The seventh, *Al-Hilliyûn*, "Footstool of the Throne;"
And, each and every one,
Sphere above sphere, and treasure over treasure,
The great decree of God made for reward and pleasure.

Saith the Perspicuous Book:*
"Look up to Heaven! look!
Dost thou see flaw or fault
In that vast vault,
Spangled with silvery lamps of night,
Or gilded with glad light
Of sunrise, or of sunset, or warm noon?
Rounded He well the moon?
Kindled He wisely the red Lord of Day?
Look twice! look thrice, and say!"

---

* Cf. Korân, lxvii. chapter "Of the Kingdom."

> Thy weak gaze fails;
> Eyesight is drowned in yon abyss of blue;
> Ye see the glory, but ye see not through:
> God's greatness veils
> Its greatness by its greatness—all that wonder
> Lieth the lowest of those Heavens under,
> Beyond which Angels view
> Allah, and Allah's mighty works, asunder;
> The thronged clouds whisper of it when they thunder.

Allah Kabír! in silence we
Meditate on Thy majesty.

39

Al-Háfiz! O "Preserver!" succor us
Who humbly trustful, cry unto Thee thus.

By the Sky and the Night star!
By Al-Târek the white star!
    Shining clear—
When darkness covers man and beast—
    To proclaim dawn near,
And the gold sun hastening from the east,
We have set a guard upon you, every one;
    Be ye not afraid!
Of seed from loins, and milk from bosom-bone,
    Ye were made:
We are able to remake you, when ye die,
    For cold death
Cometh forth from Us, as warm life cometh
    And gift of breath.
Do the darkness and the terror plot against you?
    We also plan;
They that love you are stronger than your haters
    Trust God, O man! *

" Ya Háfiz!" on your doors ye grave;
In your hearts, too, these scriptures have!

---

* Cf. Korân lxxxvi. chapter " Of the Night Star."

40

*Praise Al-Mukît, the great "Maintainer!" He
Made us, and makes our sustenance to be.*

THE chapter of the "Inevitable:"* We gave
The life ye live; why doubt ye We can save
   What once hath been from wasting—if We will—
When, like dry corn, man lieth in his grave?

Did ye cause seed to grow, or was it We,—
Wherefrom spring all the many lives that be?
   Who stirred the pulse which couples man and maid,
And in the fruit hid that which forms the tree?

Ye go afield to scatter grain, and then
Sleep, while We change it into bread for men;
   Have ye bethought why seed should shoot, not sand,
Granite, or gravel? Why the gentle rain

Falleth so clean and sweet from out Our sky,
Which might be salt and black and bitter? Why
   The soft clouds gather it from off the seas
To spread it o'er the pastures by and by?

The flame ye strike rubbing Afâr and Markh,†
Have ye considered that strange yellow spark?
   Did ye conceive such marvel, or did We
Grant it, to warm and cheer men in the dark?

---

   * Korân, lvi.
   † The woods used by the ancient Arabs to kindle fire.

SURA "OF THE INEVITABLE."

Not now, but when the soul comes to the neck,
The meaning of those mercies each shall reck.
 Then are We nearest, though ye see it not;
Can ye that summoned spirit order back?

Nay, Al-Mukît! in life and death
Thine are we: Truth Thy Scripture saith.

41

*Laud Him as "Reckoner," casting up th' account,
And makiny little merits largely mount.*

> GIVE more than thou takest:
>   If one shall salute thee,
>   Saying, "Peace be upon thee,"
>   The salute which thou makest,
>   Speak it friendlier still,
>   As beseemeth goodwill;
>   Saying, "Peace, too, and love
>   From Allah above
>   Be with thee:"—for heard
>   Is each brotherly word;
>   And it shall not be lost
>   That thou gavest him most.*

---

*Ya Hasîb! praise to Thee; for all
Our good deeds needs must be so small.*

---

* Cf. Korân, iv. chapter "Of Women."

42

Al-Jamil! "*the Benign;*" *ah, name most dear,*
Which bids us love and worship without fear.

Too much ye tremble, too much fear to feel
That yearning love which Allah's laws reveal;
Too oft forget—your troubled journey through—
He who is Power, is Grace and Beauty too,
And Clemency, and Pity, and Pure Rest,
The Highest and the Uttermost and Best;
Sweeter than honey, and more dear to see
Than any loveliness on land or sea
By bard or lover praised, or famed in story;
For these were shadows of His perfect glory;
Which is not told, because, who sees God near
Loseth the speech to speak, in loving fear,
So joyous is he, so astonishĕd.

 Hath there come to ye what the Dervish said
At Kaisareya, in the marble shrine,
Who woke from vision of the love divine?
"I have seen Allah!" quoth he—all a-glow
With splendor of the dream which filled him so—
"Yea! I have paced the Garden of Delight,
And heard and known!"

     "Impart to us thy light,"
His fellows cried.

     He paused, and smiled, and spake:
"Fain would I say it, brothers, for your sake

For I have wandered in a sphere so bright,
Have heard such things, and witnessed such a sight,
That now I know whither all nature turns,
And what the love celestial is which burns,
At the great heart of all the world, ensuring
That griefs shall pass and joy be all enduring.
Yet ask me not! I am as one who came
Where, among roses, one bush, all aflame
By fragrant crimson blossoms, charged the air
With loveliness and perfume past compare.
Then had I thought to load my skirt with roses,
That ye might judge what wealth that land discloses;
And filled my robe, plucking the peerless blooms;
But ah! the scent so rich, so heavenly, comes;
So were my senses melted into bliss
With the intoxicating breath of this;
I let the border of my mantle fall—
The roses slipped! I bring ye none at all."

---

*Brothers! with other eyes must we
Behold the Roses on that Tree.*

43

*Allah-al-Karîm! Bountiful Lord! we bless
By this good name Thy loving kindnesses.*

O MAN! what hath beguiled,
    That thou shouldst stray
    From the plain easy way
Of Allah's service, being Allah's child?
    When thou wert not,
    And when thou wast a clot,
He did foresee thee, and did fashion thee
    From heel to nape,
    Giving thee this fair shape,
Composing thee in wondrous symmetry—
More than thy mother—in the form thou wearest;
Nearer to thee than what on earth is nearest.
    Kinder than kin is He—
    Wilt thou forgetful be?*

---

*Ya Karîm! since Thou lovest thus,
Quicken, ah, quicken love in us.*

---

* Cf. Korân, lxxxii. chapter "Of Cleaving Asunder."

44

Allah-al-Rakîb! praise ye "the Watchful One,"
Who noteth what men do and leave undone.

THE book of the wicked is in Sijjîn,
   A close-writ book:
A book to be unfolded on the Awful Day,
   The day whereto men would not look.

   What Sijjîn is
  Who shall make thee know?
The Black Gaol. Under *Jehannum*,
  Under *Lathâ*, the "red glow,"
  Under *Hutamah*, "the fires which split;"
  Beneath *Sa'hîr*, the "Yellow Hell,"
  And scorching *Sakar*, lieth it,
  And *Jahîm*, where devils dwell:
  Lower from light and bliss
  Than *Hâwiyeh*, "the abyss:"
  Sijjîn is this.

But the books of the righteous are in Hilliyûn,
  And what shall make thee see
The glory of that region, nigh to God,
  Where those records be?
Joy shall make their portion: they shall lie
  With the light of delight upon their faces,
On soft seats reclining
  In peaceful places;

Drinking wine, pure wine, sealed wine,
  Whose seal is musk and rose;
Allayed by the crystal waves that shine
  In Tasmín, which flows
From the golden throne of God:—at its brink
  Angels drink.*

———

*O "Watcher!" grant our names may be
In that Book lying near to Thee.*

---

* Cf. Korân, lxxxiii. chapter "Of Short Weight."

45

Allah-al-Mujíb, Who biddest men to pray,
And hearest prayer; thus praise we Thee alway.

OUR Lord the Prophet (peace to him!) doth write—
Sura the seventeenth, intituled "Night:"—
" Pray at the noon, pray at the sinking sun,
In night-time pray; but most when night is done,
For daybreak's prayer is surely borne on high
By Angels changing guard within the sky."
And in another verse, "Dawn's prayer is more
Than the wide world with all its treasured store."

Therefore the Faithful, when the growing light.
Gives to discern a black hair from a white.
Haste to the mosque, and, bending Mecca-way,
Recite *Al-Fátihah* while 'tis scarce yet day:
Praise be to Allah, Lord of all that live.
Merciful King and Judge, to Thee we give
Worship and honor! Succor us and guide
Where those have walked who rest Thy Throne beside;
The way of peace, the way of truthful speech,
The way of righteousness. So we beseech."
He who saith this, before the east is red,
A hundred prayers of Azan hath he said.

Hear now this story of it—told, I ween,
For your soul's comfort by Jelalu-'d-deen

ALI AND THE JEW.

In the great pages of the Mesnevî;
For therein, plain and certain, shall ye see
How precious is the prayer at break of day
In Allah's ears, and in His sight alway
How sweet are reverence and gentleness
Done to His creatures:—"Ali" (whom I bless!),
The son of Abu Talib—he, surnamed
"Lion of God," in many battles famed,
The cousin of our Lord the Prophet (grace
Be his!), uprose betimes one morn, to pace,
As he was wont, unto the mosque, wherein
Our Lord (bliss live with him!) watched to begin
Al-Fâtihah. Darkling was the sky, and strait
The lane between the city and mosque-gate,
By rough stones broken and deep pools of rain;
And therethrough toilfully, with steps of pain,
Leaning upon his staff an old Jew went
To synagogue, on pious errand bent;
For those be "People of the Book," and some
Are chosen of Allah's will who have not come
Unto full light of knowledge; therefore, he,
Ali, the Caliph of proud days to be—
Knowing this good old man, and why he stirred
Thus early, ere the morning mills were heard—
Out of his nobleness and grace of soul
Would not thrust past, though the Jew blocked the whole
Breadth of the lane, slow hobbling. So they went,
That ancient first; and, in soft discontent,
After him Ali, noting how the sun
Flared near, and fearing prayer might be begun;
Yet no command upraising, no harsh cry
To stand aside, because the dignity

Of silver hairs is much, and morning praise
Was precious to the Jew, too. Thus their ways
Wended the pair; great Ali, sad and slow,
Following the graybeard, while the east, a-glow,
Blazed with bright spears of gold athwart the blue,
And the Muezzin's call came, "*Illahu!
Allah-il-Allah!*"

                In the mosque, our Lord
(On whom be peace) stood by the mimbar-board,
In act to bow and *Fátihah* forth to say.
But, while his lips moved, some strong hand did lay
Over his mouth a palm invisible,
So that no voice on the assembly fell.
Ya! Rabbi 'lalamîna—thrice he tried
To read, and thrice the sound of reading died,
Stayed by this unseen touch. Thereat amazed,
Our Lord Muhammad turned, arose, and gazed,
And saw—alone of all within the shrine—
A splendid Presence, with large eyes divine
Beaming, and golden pinions folded down,
Their speed still tokened by the fluttered gown:
Gabriel he knew, the Spirit who doth stand
Chief of the Sons of Heav'n, at God's right hand;
"Gabriel! why stay'st thou me?" the Prophet said,
"Since at this hour *the Fátihah* should be read."
But the bright Presence, smiling, pointed where
Ali towards the outer gate drew near,
Upon the threshold shaking off his shoes,
And giving "alms of entry," as men use.
"Yea!" spake th' Archangel, "sacred is the sound
Of morning praise, and worth the world's great round,
Though earth were pearl and silver; therefore I
Stayed thee, Muhammad, in the act to cry.

ALI AND THE JEW.

Lest Ali, tarrying in the lane, should miss,
For his good deed, its blessing and its bliss."
Thereat the Archangel vanished, and our Lord
Read *Fátihah* forth beneath the mimbar-board.

Us, too, Mujíb! in hearing keep;
Better is prayer than food or sleep!

46.

"All-Comprehending One," Al-Wasi'h! we
By this name also praise and honor Thee.

TURN, wheresoe'er ye be, to Mecca's stone,
   For this is holy, and your Lord doth hear;
Thitherwards turn!—so hath all Islâm one
   Heart to its thought and harbor of its prayer.

But Allah's house eastwards and westwards lies,
   Northwards and southwards. He is everywhere:
Whithersoever way ye bend your eyes,
   Face to face are ye with Al-Wasi'h there.

It is not righteousness to kneel aright
   Fronting the *Kiblah;* but to rightly hold
Of God, and of His judgment, and the bright
   Bands of His Angels; and what truth is told

In the sure Korân by God's holy Prophet;
   To succor orphans, strangers, suppliants, kin;
Your gold and worldly treasure—to give of it
   Ransom for captives, alms which mercy win:

To keep your covenants when ye covenant;
   Your woes and sufferings patiently to bear,
Being the will of God:—this is to front
   Straight for the *Kiblah:* this is faith and fear.*

Abounding Lord! in every place
Is built the Mecca of Thy grace.

---

* Cf. Korân, ii. chapter "Of the Cow."

47

*Al-Hákim! Judge of all the judges! show
Mercy to us and make us justice know.*

ONLY one Judge is just, for only One
Knoweth the hearts of men; and hearts alone
Are guilty or are guiltless. That which lied
Was not the tongue—he is a red dog tied.

And that which slew was not the hand ye saw
Grasping the knife—she is a slave whose law
The master gives, seated within the tent;
The hand was handle to the instrument;

The dark heart murdered. O believers! leave
Judgment to Heav'n—except ye do receive
Office and order to accomplish this;
Then honorable, and terrible, it is.

The Prophet said:* "At the great day of doom
Such fear on the most upright judge shall come
That he shall moan, 'Ah! would to God that I
Had stood for trial, and not sate to try!'"

He said: "The Angels of the Scales will bring
Just and unjust who judged before Heav'n's King,
Grasping them by the neck; and, if it be,
One hath adjudged his fellows wickedly,

---

* Cf. the Mishkát-ul-Masábíh.

"He shall be hurled to hell so vast a height
'Tis forty years' fierce journey ere he light;
But if one righteously hath borne the rod,
The Angels kiss those lips which spake for God."

———

*Lord! make us just, that we may be
A little justified with Thee.*

48

"*The Loving*"—*Al-Wadood!* ah, title dear,
Whereby Thy children praise Thee, free of fear.

SWEET seem your wedded days; and dear and tender
  Your children's talk; brave 'tis to hear the tramp
Of pastured horses; and to see the splendor
  Of gold and silver plunder; and to camp

With goats and camels by the bubbling fountain;
  And to drink fragrance from the desert wind,
And to sit silent on the mighty mountain;
  And all the joys which make life bright and kind.

But ye have heard of streams more brightly flowing
  Than those whereby ye wander; of a life
Glorious and glad and pure beyond earth's knowing;
  Love without loss, and wealth without the strife.

Lo! we have told you of the golden Garden
  Kept for the Faithful, where the soil is still
Wheat-flour and musk and camphire, and fruits harden
  To what delicious savor each man will

Upon the Tooba tree; which bends its cluster
  To him that doth desire, bearing all meat;
And of the sparkling fountains which out-lustre
  Diamonds and emeralds, running clear and sweet,

Tasmín and Salsabíl, whose lucent waters
  Are rich, delicious, undistracting wine;
And of the Houris, pleasure's perfect daughters,
  Virgins of Paradise, whose black eyes shine

Soul-deep with love and languor, having tresses
  Night-dark, with scents of the gold-blooming date
And scarlet roses; lavishing caresses
  That satisfy, but never satiate;

Whose looks refrain from any save their lover,
  Whose peerless limbs and bosoms' ivory swell
Are like the ostrich egg which feathers cover
  From stain and dust, so white and rounded well:

Dwelling in marvellous pavilions, builded
  Of hollow pearls, wherethrough a great light shines—
Cooled by soft breezes and by glad suns gilded—
  On the green pillows where the Blest reclines.

A rich reward it shall be, a full payment
  For life's brief trials and sad virtue's stress,
When friends with friends, clad all in festal raiment,
  Share in deep Heaven the Angels' happiness;

Nay, and full payment, though ye give those pleasures
  Which make life dear, to fight and die for faith,
Rendering to God your wives and flocks and treasures,
  That He may pay you tenfold after death.

For, if the bliss of Paradise, transcending
  Delights of earth, should win ye to be bold,
Yet know, this glory hath its crown and ending
  In Allah's grace, which is the Joy untold,

The Utmost Bliss. Beyond the Happy River
The justified shall see God's face in Heaven,
Live in His sweet goodwill,* and taste for ever
Al-Wadood's † love, unto His children given.

*Yea! for high Heaven's felicity
Is but the shadow, Lord, of Thee.*

---

* Cf. Korân, ix. chapter " Of Repentance."
† Cf. Korân, lxxxv. chapter " Of Zodiacal Signs."

49

Al-Majîd! Glorious Lord upon the Throne,*
With this great name we praise Thee, Sovereign One!

By the Heavens, walled with silver signs and towers!
      By the Promised Day!
By the Witness and the Witnessed; and the Way
Of righteousness!—this glorious Book of ours
      Lieth treasured up in Heaven,
      As 'twas given
On the mighty "Night of Powers;"
      And its easy bond is this,
      The which to keep is bliss:
      "None save Glorious Allah serve;
      Never from His precepts swerve;
      Honor teacher, father, mother;
      Unto him who is thy brother,
      Unto kindred, friends also,
      Orphans, suppliants, sad ones, show
      Gentleness and help; to each
      Speak with kind and courteous speech.
      Give in alms that thou may'st spare,
      And be constant in thy prayer."*

Allah al-Majîd! Thy favor grant,
That we may keep this covenant.

---

* Cf. Korân, lxxxv. chapter "Of Celestial Signs.,"
† Cf. Korân, ii. chapter "Of the Heifer."

50

*Al-Bâhith! Opener of the Tombs! we praise
Thy power, which unto life the dead can raise.*

Iblîs spake to Abraham:
"What is this thy Lord hath told thee?
Shall the Resurrection be
When the mouldering clods enfold thee?
Nay! and if a man might rise,
Buried whole, in heedful wise,
See yon carcase, tempest-beaten—
Part the wandering fox hath eaten,
Part by fishes hath been torn,
Part the sea-fowl hence have borne;
Never back those fragments can
Come to him who was a man."

Abraham spake unto his Lord:*
" Show me how is wrought this wonder;
Can Thy resurrection be
When a man's dust lies asunder?"

"Art thou therefore not believing,"
Allah said, "because deceiving
Iblîs fills with lies thy heart?"
"Nay," he answered, "but impart
Knowledge, Mightiest One and Best!
That my heart may be at rest."

---

* Cf. Korân, ii. chapter "Of the Heifer."

God said: "Take, thou doubting one!
Four birds from among My creatures;
Sever each bird's head, and so
Mingle feathers, forms, and features,
That the fragments shall not be
Knowable to such as ye.
Into four divide the mass,
Then upon the mountains pass,
On four peaks a portion lay,
And, returning homeward, say,
'By the name and power of God—
Who hath made men of the clod,
And hath said the dead shall rise—
Birds! fly hither in such wise
As ye lived.' And they shall come,
Perfect, whole, and living, home."

Thereupon Al-Khalîl took
A raven, eagle, dove, and cock;
From their bodies shore the heads,
Cut the four fowl into shreds,
Mingled all their mass together,
Blood and bone, and flesh and feather;
Then dividing this four-wise,
Laid it where four peaks did rise
Two to south and two to north.
Then the dove's head held he forth,
Crying, "Come!" Lo! at the word
Cooed at his feet the slaughtered bird.
"Come, raven!" spake he: as he spoke,
On glossy wing, with eager croak,
Flew round the raven. Then he said,
"Return! thou cock:" the cock obeyed.

Lastly the eagle summoned he,
Which circling came, on pinions free,
Restored and soaring to the sky,
With perfect plumes and undimmed eye.

So in the Holy Book 'tis writ
How Abraham's heart at rest was set.

Why should we fear to yield our breath,
To Thee That art the Lord of Death?

51

*Ash-Shahîd! God is "Witness!" and He took
Witness of us, ye People of the Book!*

THE spirits of the Prophets came at morn
    To Sinai, summoned by their Lord's command,
Singers and seers;—those born and those unborn,
    The chosen souls of men, a solemn band.

The noble army ranged, in viewless might,
    Around that mountain peak which pierces heaven;
Greater and lesser teachers, sons of light;
    Their number was ten thousand score and seven.

Then Allah took a covenant with His own,
    Saying, "My wisdom and My word receive;
Speak of Me unto men, known or unknown,
    Heard or unheard; bid such as will, believe."

"And there shall come apostles, guiding ye,
    Jesus, Muhammad: follow them and aid!
Are you resolved, and will you war for Me?"
    "We are resolved, O Lord of all!" they said.

"Bear witness then!" spake Allah, "souls most dear,
    I am your Lord and ye heralds of Mine."
Thenceforward through all lands His Prophets bear
    The message of the mystery divine.*

*Allah-ash-Shahîd! make us to hear
The errand that Thy children bear.*

---

* Cf. Korân, iii. chapter "Of Imran's Family."

52

O Thou, the Truth! when so Thy name we call,
All's said that need be said, sith Thou art all.

TRUTH and all truth He is! serve Him alone
.Who hath none other by nor near His Throne;
Unto all sins is Allah's pardon given
Except what giveth Him partners in Heaven,*
Being Apart, Exalted, Truth and Light,
Only and wholly—hold thou this aright!

Ya Hakk! true God! never with Thee
Can other or can equal be.

---

* Cf. Korân, iv. chapter "Of Women."

53

Alai kul shay Wakîl! * *Guardian of all!*
By this name trustfully on Thee we call.

VERILY God is guard!
What other hath created you, and made
Men gone before, and earth's foundations laid
　　So broad and hard,
To be your dwelling-place;
And Heaven's star-jewelled face
Arched for your roof-top; and the tender rain
Sent down at the due season, whereby grain
　　Groweth, and clustered gold
　　Of dates, and grapes that hold
The purple and the amber honey-juice?
　　These for your use
　　Your Lord and "Agent" gave.
Make Him no peers, nor other guardian have.

Allah-al-Wakîl! Thy wards are we;
Have us in Thy fidelity.

---

* Cf. Korân, ii. chapter "Of the Heifer."

54

*Thou mighty One! Whose mercy hath upraised
Mankind to praise Thee, be Thou hereby praised!*

CONSIDER them that serve
The false gods, how they lay in golden dishes
Honey and fruits and fishes
Before their idols; and the green fly comes,
Shoots through the guarded gates, and hums
Scorn of their offering, stealing what she will;
And none of these great gods the thief can kill,
    So swift she is and small:
    And none of all
Can make one little fly, for all their state;
So feeble are they, and so falsely great.*
Ye people of the stocks and stones! herein
A parable is set against your sin.
But Allah high doth rule
Whose hand made all things, being "Powerful."

---

*Al-Kawî! King of power and might!
Be Thy hand o'er us day and night!*

---

* Cf. Korân, xxii. chapter "Of Believers."

55

Allah-al-Mateen! "*Firm*" *is our Lord and fast;*
Praise Him Who doth uphold Thee to the last.

    By the Angels ranged in ranks,
    And the Rain-cloud Drivers,
And the Reciters of the word, "Thy God is one,"
    Firm is our Lord!
    Of the heavens the tent-pole,
    Al-Watad; and of earth
    Habl-al-Mateen, the sure Cord:*
    By this thy soul
    Holdeth, from birth:
Fast is the cord, and sure;
They only shall endure
Who dwell beneath the mighty tent upholden
By *Al-Watad,*† the Golden.

Stay of Thy servants, Al-Mateen!
In Thee is strong deliverance seen.

---

* Cf. Korân, iii. chapter "Of the Family of Imran."
† Cf. Korân, lxxviii. chapter "Of the Information."

56

*Al-Walî ! Nearest of all friends, and Best,
So praise your Lord, Whose help is mightiest.*

CLOSE is He always to His faithful ones,
But closer dwelt they in the times of old.
Hath it come to ye what Al-Baidhâwi
Presenteth of the days of Abraham,
Whom Allah called His "Friend," and like a friend
Softly entreated,* stooping out of Heaven
To help and comfort him so dear to God?
Ofttimes the Angels of his Lord would light
Familiarly, with folded wings, before
The curtain of his tent, conversing there;
Ofttimes, on thorny flats of wilderness,
Or in the parched pass, or the echoing cave,
The very voice of God would thrill his ears;
And he might answer, as a man with man,
Hearing and speaking things unspeakable.
Wherefore, no marvel that he gave his son
At Allah's bidding, and had back his son—
Patient and safe—when the wild goat came down
And hung amid the nebbuk by his horns,
On Thabîr, nigh to Mecca, in the vale
Of Mina;† and the knife of Abraham
Reddened with unwept blood.

---

* Cf. Korân, iv. chapter "Of Women."
† Cf. Korân, xxxvii. chapter "Of the Ranged."

                          There had fall'n drought
Upon the land, and all the mouths he fed
Hungered for meal; therefore Al-Khalîl sent
Messengers unto Egypt—to a lord
Wealthy and favorable, having store
Of grain and cattle by the banks of Nile.
"Give unto Abraham," the message said,
"A little part for gold, yet more for love—
(As he had given, if the strait were thine)
Meal of the millet, lentil, wheat, and bean,
That he and his may live; for drought hath come
Upon our fields and pastures, and we pine."
Spake the Egyptian lord, "Lo! now ye ask
O'ermuch of me for friendliness, and more
Than gold can buy, since dearth hath also come
Over our fields, and nothing is to spare.
Yet had it been to succor Abraham,
And them that dwell beneath his tent, the half
Of all we hold had filled your empty sacks.
But he will feed people we wot not of,
Poor folk, and hungry wanderers of the waste:
The which are nought to us, who have of such,
If there were surplusage. Therefore return;
Find food elsewhere!"

                           Then said the messengers
One to another, "If we shall return
With empty sacks, our master's name, so great
For worship in the world, will suffer shame,
And men will say he asked and was denied."
Therefore they filled their sacks with white sea-sand
Gathered by Gaza's wave, and sorrowfully
Journeyed to Kedar, where lay Abraham,
To whom full privately they told this thing,

ABRAHAM'S BREAD. 117

Saying, "We filled the sacks with snow-white sand,
Lest thy great name be lessened 'mongst the folk,
Seeing us empty-handed; for the man
Denied thee corn; since thou wouldst give, quoth he,
To poor folk and to wanderers of the waste,
And there are hungry mouths enough by Nile."

Then was the heart of Abraham sore, because
The people of his tribe drew round to share
The good food brought, and all the desert trooped
With large-eyed mothers and their pining babes,
Certain of succor if the sheikh could help.
So did the spirit of Al-Khalîl sink
That into swoon he fell, and lay as one
Who hath not life. But Sarai, his wife—
That knew not—bade her maidens bring a sack,
Open its mouth, and knead some meal for cakes.
And when the sack was opened, there showed flour,
Fine, three times bolted, whiter than sea-sand;
Which in the trough they kneaded, rolling cakes,
And baking them over the crackling thorns;
So that the savor spread throughout the camp
Of new bread smoking, and the people drew
Closer and thicker, as ye see the herds
Throng—horn, and wool, and hoof—at watering-time,
When after fiery leagues, the wells are reached.

But Abraham, awaking, smelled the bread:
"Whence," spake he unto Sarai, "hast thou meal,
Wife of my bosom? for the smell of bread
Riseth, and lo! I see the cakes are baked."
"By God! Who is the only One," she said,
"Whence should it come save from thy friend who sent,
The lord of Egypt?" "Nay!" quoth Abraham,

And fell upon his face, low-worshipping,
"But this hath come from the dear mighty hands
Of Allah—of the Lord of Egypt's lords—
My 'Friend,' and King, and Helper: now my folk
Shall live and die not. Glory be to God!"

He that hath Allah for a friend,
To want and woe hath put the end.

57

*Rich to reward your Lord is; oh, do ye
Praise Al-Hamíd, the "Ever-praiseworthy!"*

PRAISE him by alms; and when ye help believers,
    Mar not your gifts with grudging word or will;
Since ye at Allah's hands are free receivers,
    Freely bestow. A garden on a hill

Is as a likeness of that fair compassion
    Shown for the sake of God: the heavy rain
Descendeth, and the dew; and every fashion
    Of good seed springs tenfold in fruit and grain.

The likeness of the evil heart, bestowing
    That men may praise, is as the thin-clad peak,
Wherefrom the rain washes all soil for growing,
    Leaving the hard rock naked, fruitless, bleak.

Say, will ye plant on rock or plenteous garden?
    Grow nought, or grow green vines that shade afford?—
Forgive your brethren as ye ask for pardon;
    Give as ye have received, and praise your Lord!*

---

*Allah-al-Hamíd! what tongue can tell
Thy goodness, ever-laudable?*

---

*Cf. Korân ii. chapter "Of the Heifer."

58

Al-Múshi! The "Accountant!" laud Him so
Who reckoneth up the deeds men do below.

"IN GOD'S NAME, MERCIFUL, COMPASSIONATE!"

WHEN Earth shall quake with quaking,*
And cast her burden forth
Of corpses; and live men
Shall ask—with terror shaking—
"What aileth Earth?" that day
She shall reply, and say
    That which her Lord commands:
    And men shall come in bands,
This side and that side, ranged to show
Their works, and the account to know.
And he that wrought of good a red ant's weight
    Shall see it writ:
And who did evil, aye! as the skin of a date,
    Shall witness it.

Al-Múhsi! dread Accountant! look
In mercy on our judgment-book.

---

* Cf. Korân, xcix. chapter "Of the Earthquake."

59

Al-Mubdî! praise Him by this holy name,
Who gave to all the spark which lights life's flame.

WHENCE came ye; and the people of the groves;
The streams, the seas, the wilderness, the air;
Beasts, fishes, fowl; each with their lives and loves,
Each glad to be, each in its kind so fair?

"Begotten of their like?" Yea! but "their like,"
Who did devise that, and the hidden charm
Whereby—as flame from torch to torch doth strike—
The light of life shines on, bright, joyous, warm?

Al-Mubdî hath devised it! His decree
In the beginning shaped and ordered each,
Saying to all these things foreseen, "So be!"
And so they were, obeying Allah's speech.

Al-Mubdî! " Great Beginner!" take
Our praises, for life's pleasant sake!

60

He made life—and He takes it—but instead
Gives more; praise the Restorer, Al-Muʻhîd!

HE who died at Azan sends
This to comfort faithful friends.

   Faithful friends! it lies, I know,
Pale and white and cold as snow;
And ye say, "Abdullah's dead!"
Weeping at my feet and head;
I can see your falling tears,
I can hear your cries and prayers;
Yet I smile, and whisper this—
"I am not that thing you kiss;
Cease your tears, and let it lie;
It *was* mine, it is not I."

   Sweet friends! what the women lave,
For its last bed in the grave,
Is a tent which I am quitting,
Is a garment no more fitting,
Is a cage from which, at last,
Like a hawk my soul hath passed.
Love the inmate, not the room;
The wearer, not the garb; the plume
Of the falcon, not the bars
Which kept him from the splendid stars.

A MESSAGE FROM THE DEAD.

Loving friends! be wise, and dry
Straightway every weeping eye;
What ye lift upon the bier
Is not worth a wistful tear.
'Tis an empty sea-shell, one
Out of which the pearl is gone;
The shell is broken, it lies there;
The pearl, and all, the soul, is here.
'Tis an earthen jar whose lid
Allah sealed, the while it hid
That treasure of His treasury,
A mind which loved Him; let it lie!
Let the shard be earth's once more,
Since the gold shines in His store!

Allah Mu'híd, Allah most good!
Now thy grace is understood;
Now my heart no longer wonders
What Al-Barsakh * is, which sunders
Life from death, and death from Heaven;
Nor the "Paradises Seven"
Which the happy dead inherit;
Nor those "birds" which bear each spirit
Towards the Throne, " green birds and white,"
Radiant, glorious, swift their flight!
Now the long, long darkness ends,
Yet ye wail, my foolish friends,
While the man whom ye call "dead"
In unbroken bliss instead
Lives, and loves you; lost, 'tis true
By any light which shines for you;
But in light ye cannot see
Of unfulfilled felicity,

---

* Cf. Korân, xxiii. chapter "Of Believers."

And enlarging Paradise,
Lives the life that never dies.

   Farewell, friends! Yet not farewell;
Where I am, ye too shall dwell.
I am gone before your face
A heart-beat's time, a gray ant's pace.
When ye come where I have stepped,
Ye will marvel why ye wept,
Ye will know, by true love taught,
That here is all, and there is naught.
Weep awhile, if ye are fain,
Sunshine still must follow rain!
Only not at death, for death—
Now I see—is that first breath
Which our souls draw when we enter
Life, that is of all life centre.

   Know ye Allah's law is love,
Viewèd from Allah's Throne above:
Be ye firm of trust, and come
Faithful onward to your home!
"*La Allah illa Allah!* Yea,
Mu'hîd! Restorer! Sovereign!" say!

He who died at Azan gave
This to those that made his grave.

61

*Al-Moʻhyî! the " Quickener!" hereby
Praise Him Whom Angels praise eternally.*

" AND of His signs is this,"* saith the Great Book;
" Under the angry sun the slain earth—look!—
Dries up to dust; dies every growing thing;
Then blow we breaths of southern wind which bring
Rain-dropping clouds, and see! the dead earth lives,
And stirs, and swells; and every herb revives.
So shall the dead be quickened by His breath,
This is Al-Moʻhyî's sign," the Great Book saith.

*O thou believer! shall it be
He saves the green thing, and not thee?*

---

* Cf. Korân, xli. chapter " Of Signs Explained."

62

He quickeneth, but " He killeth:" blessed they
Who may abide in trust that final day!

YEA! some have found right good to hear the summons
   of their Lord,
And gone as glad as warriors proud, who take up spear
   and sword
At sounding of the song of fight; as light of heart as
   those
For whom the bride unveileth her mouth of pearl and
   rose.

Jelalu-'d-'Din, Er-Rumi, the saint of Balkh, the son
Of him surnamed "Flower of the Faith," this was a
   chosen one,
To whom Death softly showed himself, Heaven's gentle
   call to give;
For what word is it bids us die, save that which made
   us live?

Sick lay he there in Konya; 'twas dawn; the golden
   stream
Of light, new springing in the east, on his thin lips did
   gleam—

THE ANGEL OF DEATH.

Those lips which spake the praise of God all through
    his holy years,
And murmured now, with faith and hope unchanged,
    the morning prayers.

Then one who watched beside his bed, heard at the
    inner gate
A voice cry, "*Aftah!* 'open!' from far I come, and
    wait
To speak my message to Jelâl—a message that will
    bring
Peace and reward to him who lies the *Fâtihah* mur-
    muring."

Thereat the watcher drew the bar which closed the
    chamber-door,
Wondering and 'feared, for ne'er was heard upon this
    earth before
Accents so sweet and comforting, nor ever eyes of men
Saw presence so majestical as his who entered then.

Entered with gliding footsteps a bright celestial youth,
Splendid and strange in beauty, past words to speak its
    truth;
Midnight is not so dark and deep as was his solemn
    gaze,
By love and pity lighted, as the night with silvery
    rays.

"What is thy name?" the watcher asked, "that I may
    tell my lord,
Thou fair and dreadful messenger! whose glance is as
    a sword;

Whose face is like the Heaven unveiled; whose tender searching voice
Maketh the heart cease beating, but bids the soul rejoice."

"AZRAEL ANA," spake the shape, "I am the Spirit of Death;
And I am sent from Allah's throne to stay thy master's breath."
"Come in! come in! thou Bird of God," cried joyously Jelâl,
"Fold down thy heavenly plumes and speak!—Islâm! what shall be, shall."

"Thou blessed one!" the Angel said, "I bring thy time of peace;
When I have touched thee on the eyes, life's latest ache will cease;
God bade me come as I am seen amid the heavenly host,
No enemy of awful mould, but he who loveth most."

"Dear Angel! do what thou art bid," quoth Jelâl, smilingly,
"God willing, thou shalt find to-day a patient one in me;
Sweet is the cup of bitterness which cometh in such wise!"
With that he bowed his saintly brow,—and Azrael kissed his eyes.

Al-Mumît! " *Slayer!*" *send Him thus,*
In love, not anger, unto us.

63

*Praise Him, Al-Haiy! the "Ever-living" King,
Who to eternal life His own doth bring.*

SAITH the Book: "Count not as dead *
Such as for the Faith have bled;
Stark and red their bodies lie,
But their souls are in the sky,
Resident with God, who grants
All for which the spirit pants.
Joyful are they, resting there
Free from sorrow, pain, or fear;
Watching us who, left in life,
Are not quit, as yet, of strife;
But shall soon attain, to share
Allah's mercies, and declare—
Side by side with those—that He
Showeth grace eternally,
And withholdeth not the pay
At the ending of the day.

*Ya-Haiy! Thou ever-living Lord,
Be ours such work and such reward.*

---

* Cf. Korân, iii. chapter "Of Imran's Family."

64

Magnify Him, Al-Kaiyum; and so call
The " Self-subsisting" God Who judgeth all.

WHEN the trumpet shall sound,
    On that day,*
The wicked, slow-gathering,
    Shall say,
"Is it long we have lain in our graves?
    For it seems as an hour!"
Then will Israfil call them to judgment;
    And none shall have power
To turn aside, this way or that;
    And their voices will sink
To silence, except for the sounding
    Of a noise, like the noise on the brink
Of the sea, when its stones
    Are dragged with a clatter and hiss
Down the shore, in the wild breakers' roar:
    The sound of their woe shall be this!

Then they who denied
    That He liveth Eternal, "Self-made,"
Shall call to the mountains to crush them;
    Amazed and affrayed.

Thou Self-subsistent, Living Lord!
Thy grace against that day afford.

---

* Cf. Korân, xx. chapter "Of T. H."

SURA "OF DAYBREAK."

65

Al-Wâjid! praise hereby that Watchful One
Whose eyes see all things underneath the sun.

By the Ten holy eves and the Dawns of gold!*
By the One and the Manifold!
By the deepening of the Darkness of the night!
(And these be oaths of might:)
Hast thou considered what with Ad God wrought,
And whereunto He brought
Proud Iram of the pillared throne,
Whose like no other land did own;
And Thamûd's race, which hewed houses of rocks;
And Pharaoh, strong for shocks
As is a tent with tent-pegs driven deep?†
Lo! these their haughty state did keep,
And multiply their wickedness;
Till Allah, who long-suffering hath,
Laid upon them the scourges of His wrath.

Verily, as a "watch-tower" is your Lord.
Lo! if ye knew this, would ye shut your hoard
When the poor cry; devour the weak; and love
Your riches more than treasures stored above?

---

* Cf. Korân, lxxxix. chapter "Of Daybreak."
† The Arabic word *Watad* bears this signification.

Ho! when the earth's bones crack,
And, rank on rank, the angels gather,
And hell's black gates fly back,
How will each say, "Would God in life's fair weather,
I had bethought me of this storm of hell!"

  But then it shall be well
For thee, thou soul! to-day uncomforted,
Who know'st that Allah sees;
And patiently awaitest till He please
Call thee to comfort, praising Him and praised.
Joyous thou shalt be raised
To Paradise, hearing His angels say,
"Enter, and be exceeding glad to-day!"

Al-Wâjid! *"Watcher!" save by grace,*
Who shall attain that happy place?

66

*Wâhid! The "One!" ye faithful, say herein
Sura Al-I'hlâs,* cleansing souls from sin.*

"IN GOD'S NAME, MERCIFUL, COMPASSIONATE!"

SAY: "He is God alone,
Eternal on the Throne.
Of none begotten, and begetting none,
Who hath not like unto Him any one!" †

---

*Ya Wâhid! Holy! Only! we
Thus do declare Thy unity.*

---

* This name is given to the Sura as "clearing oneself" from heresy.
† Cf. Korân, cxii. chapter "Of Unity."

67.

*As-Samad! the "Eternal!" by this name
Laud Him Who will be, was, and is the same.*

OF Heaven's prodigious years man wotteth nought;
The "Everlasting!"—hast thou strained thy thought
Searching that depth, which numbs the seeking mind
As too much light the eager gaze doth blind?
The years of men are measured by the sun,
And were not, until he his course begun;
And will not be, when his gold dial dies:
But God lived while no sun shone in the skies;
And shall be living when all worlds are dead:
Yet hereof, though ye see the truth is said,
Ye take no more the meaning than one takes
Measure of ocean by the cup that slakes
His thirst, from rillet running to the sea.

Behind—before ye, shines Eternity,
Visible as the vault's fathomless blue,
Which is so deep the glance goes never through,
Though nothing stays save depth: so is it seen
That Allah must be ever, and hath been;
Seen, but not comprehended—for man's wit
Knows this, yet knows—not understanding it.

Mete ye not Allah's times by man's: life gives
No measure of the Life Divine which lives

Unending, uncommenced, having no stay
Of yesterday, to-morrow, or to-day;
Being forever one unbroken Now
Where past and future come not.

                          Heard'st thou how,
What time fair Zion was given to sword and flame,
Ozair* the Jew upon his camel came
Over those hills which ring the sea of Lot,†
So that one footstep and—ye see her not,
And then another—and the city comes
Full upon view with all her milk-white domes.
But the Chaldean now had spoiled the place,
And desolate and waste was Zion's face,
Her proud abodes unpeopled, and her ways
Heaped with charred beams and lintels. Ozair says,
"O Lord! who promised to Jerusalem
Comfort and peace; and for her sons, to them
A glad return, how shall Thy word be kept
When fire and steel over these roofs have swept,
And she, that was a queen, lies dead and black,
A smoking ruin, where the jackals pack?
A hundred years were not enough to give
Life back to Zion! Can she ever live?"

But while he spake, the Angel of the Lord
Laid on his doubting front a fiery sword,
And Ozair in that lonely desert spot
Fell prone, and lay—breathing and moving not—
One hundred years, while the great world rolled on,
And Zion rose, and mighty deeds were done.

---

    * Identified by some commentators with Ezra of Scripture.
    † The Dead Sea.

And when the hundred years were flown, God said,
"Awake, Ozair! how long hast tarriĕd,
Thinkest thou, here?" Ozair replied, "A day,
Perchance, or half." The awful Voice said, "Nay!
But look upon thy camel." Of that beast
Nought save white bones was left: no sign, the least,
Of flesh, or hair, or hide: the desert grass
Was matted o'er its shanks, and roots did pass
From a gnarled fig-tree through the eye-pits twain,
And in and out its ribs grew the vervain.
But 'mid the moulderings of its saddle-bags
And crimson carpet, withered into rags,
A basket, full of new-picked dates, stood there
Beside a cruise of water, standing where
He set them fresh, twice fifty years ago;
And all the dates were golden with the glow
Of yestreen's sunset, and the cruise's rim
Sparkled with water to the very brim.
"Ozair!" the awful Voice spake, "look on these!
He maketh and unmaketh what shall please;
Saves or destroys, restores or casts away;
And centuries to Him are as a day;
And cities all as easy to revive
As this thy camel here, which now shall live."

Thereon the skull and bones together crept
From tangled weed and sand where they had slept;
The hide and hair came, and the flesh filled in,
The eyes returned their hollow pits within,
The saddle-bags upon its haunches hung,
The carpet on the saddle-horns was flung,
The nose-rope from the muzzle fell. The beast
Rose from its knees, and would have made to feast

On the green herbage where its bones had lain,
But that it heard bells of a caravan
Coming from Kedron, and with glad cry roared.
Then Ozair looked, and saw—newly restored—
Zion's fair walls and temples, and a crowd
Of citizens; and traffic rich and loud
In her white streets; and knew time should not be
Reckoned 'gainst Him who hath eternity.

As-Samad! Everlasting One!
Thy times are good: Thy will be done.

68

*Al-Kadar! He is " Providence!" hereby
The Lord of all things living magnify.*

WHEN ye say *Kismat*, say it wittingly,
  O true believers! under Allah's throne
Place is not left for those accursed three,
  "Destiny," "Fortune," "Chance." Allah alone

Ruleth His children: *Kismat* ye shall deem
  Each man's "allotted portion," from of old
Fixed for his part in the Eternal scheme
  By those great Hands which all the worlds enfold.

Sayeth "the Book:" "There passeth no man's soul
  Except by God's permission, and the Speech
Writ in the scroll determining the whole,
  The times of all men, and the times for each."*

Also it sayeth: "If a man shall choose
  This world's reward, to him it shall be given;
And if a man shall dare his life to lose
  For Paradise, he shall be paid in Heaven." †

---

*Ya Kadar! " Ruler!" teach us still,
Islâm, submission to Thy will.*

---

* Cf. Korân, iii. chapter " Of Imran's Family."
† Cf. Korân, ii. chapter " Of the Cow."

69

Al-Muktadir! the " Powerful !" by this
Praise we the Word, whence cometh woe and bliss.

VERILY, all things—saith "the Book"*—We made,
Decreeing; and Our bidding was one word,
Quick, as the twinkling of an eye; and all,
Whatever things men do, stands in the scrolls,
Where great and small alike are written down;
And then shall surely come the Hour—the Hour!
And bitter for the sinners it will be
When they are dragged, upon their faces, down
To hell, and taste the touch of fire; but sweet
Will it be for the pious—these shall sit
'Mid streams and gardens in the seat of truth,
Happy, near Muktadir, the Mighty One.

Grant us that seat of truth to see,
Almighty Allah! nigh to Thee.

---

* Cf. Korân, liv. chapter "Of the Moon."

70, 71

*Mukaddim ! Muwakhir ! by these names still
Praise Him Who hath forewarned, and doth fulfil.*

WHEN the trumpet shall be ringing,
Then the threatened Day hath come,
Every soul to judgment bringing.*

Each soul shall itself deliver
With two Angels, unto doom,
With a Witness and a Driver.

He that driveth shall say, "Vainly
Warned we thee, till this upholding
Of the veil: now thou seest plainly."

And the Witness by his side,
He shall say, a scroll unfolding,
"This is what I testified."

Loud shall sound th' award eternal:
"Hurl to hell the misbelievers,
Sinners, liars;—let infernal

"Torments seize perverse transgressors!"
Then will speak the wan deceivers,
Seeking pleas and intercessors.

But the awful Voice shall thunder,
"Wrangle not in Allah's hearing!
Many a sign and many a wonder

---

* Cf. Korân, 1. chapter "Of K."

SURA "OF K." 141

"Did forewarn ye of repentance;*
Time is past for more forbearing;
Not with Us is change of sentence."

Heaven shall say to Hell that morning,
"Art thou full?" Hell shall inquire,
"Hast thou others?" blackly yawning

With choked gullet. But believing
Souls will see, brought nigh and nigher,
Paradise's gates, receiving

Those to whom We promised Heaven.
"Patient ones! for ever striving
Towards the Merciful! forgiven

Are your falterings; enter ye
Into peace; now is arriving
The great Day of eternity."

---

*Forewarner and Fulfiller! we
Confess with dread Thine equity.*

---

* The text is, "I put forth unto you the menace."

72, 73, 74, 75

*Awwal! Akhir! Tháhir! Batin! these four
Be "Mothers of the Names;" * thy Lord adore,
Speaking such words as do Him truly call
Essence and Substance, First and Last in all.*

Sura the seven and fiftieth: † there is writ
The holy verse which keeps the charge of it;
   The verse which all the names of Allah holdeth
As in one sky the silver stars all sit.

The chapter "of the Iron!"—and this script
Set on its forefront, as a hilt is tipped
   With four-fold gold; or as a helm of steel
By some far-sparkling crest-gem is equipped.

"He is the First and Last"—this scripture shows—
"Outer and Inner, That which doth disclose,
   And That which hides Itself; the Manifest,
The Secret; and all things and thoughts He knows."

"In six days earth and heaven He made alone,
Then reascended the Eternal Throne;
   What entereth earth and issueth thence He sees,
And what goes up and down the sky is known"

---

  * These four divine titles are known by the technical appellation of "The Mothers of the Names," being regarded as fundamental and all-comprehensive.
  † Cf. Korân, lvii. chapter "Of Iron," v. 3.

"To Allah, Who is nigh where'er ye be,
And whatsoever deeds ye do doth see;
His is the kingdom of the earth and heaven;
All things return to Allah finally."

---

*Beginning! End! Without! Within!
We celebrate Thy praise herein.*

76

Laud Him who governs governors and kings,
Angels, and Djins, and men, and living things.

Wot ye of Solomon's signet, graved of a sapphire in gold,
  Graved with the great name of God, writ on the blue of the stone?
Wisdom and riches and power had he who that treasure did hold;
  Safe in the strength of the signet he sate on his ivory throne.

Only King Solomon knew how the dread letters did flow,
  What was the breathing of *Aleph*, where came the whispering *Yod;*
When he spake the ineffable Word, the sea-winds at bidding would blow;
  And the hills yield their iron, and jewels, and gold, at the naming of God.

And out of the void of the sky, and up from the gulfs and the capes,
  And forth from the caverns of earth, and down from the mountains of flame,
Flocked Demons with wonderful wings, and Ifreet of horrible shape,
  And Djins, with red eyes, made of fire; Divs, Peris, and Giants, they came.

SOLOMON'S SIGNET.

They came, at the call of *the name,* from Kâf, that en-
  girdles the seas;
  From the gloom of the tombs in the graveyard, from
  ruins on desolate ground;
From the pool and the marsh and the forest; from poi-
  sonous blossoms and trees;—
  Monstrous or dwarfish,—constrained, enchained, sub-
  dued, by a sound;

The sound of the title of Allah, spoken so as the Angels
  speak:—
Nor spirits uncomely only, and evil; ethereal bands
Thronged down from their heavenly houses, the Great
  King's service to seek,
  Hearing that nameless Name which all things living
  commands.

And the fowl and the beasts were fain to gather, each
  creature by each,
  When Solomon summoned hereby, pronouncing the
  mystical words.
Moreover, their dumb mouths opened, and the fly and
  the bee had a speech;
  And he knew the heart of the lions, and learned the
  mind of the birds.

Thus is it writ how he marched by Tayf from the Syrian land
  Through the "Valley of Ants" and heard the cry of
  that people of clay,
"Hide ye! hide in the earth! for there passeth Solomon's band;
  We are many and wise, but we die, if the king's foot
  cometh this way."

And he laughed, but leaped to the ground, and bowed
   his forehead and said,
   "O Lord God! grant me to learn from the ant the
   wit to be meek.
I am many and strong, and a king; yet Thou canst in-
   stantly tread
   The pride of this earth to dust, and the strongest to
   Thee are but weak!"

Then he viewed the birds, and cried, "I see not
   amongst ye here
   Al-Hudhud, the crested lapwing; what doth she to
   linger away?
Ill shall it fall for her, who seeketh us water clear,
   If she find not a fountain for prayers before the ending of day!

But they tarried not long until the whirr of her speckled
   wings
   Brought unto Solomon's feet the crested lapwing,
   who spake,
"I have seen a queen that is greater than any save thee,
   O King!
   In Seba she reigneth majestic, and glorious kingship
   doth make.

"There hath she a marvellous throne of silver, figured
   with gold,
   And the head of the throne is a moon in a jasper and
   emerald curve,
For her people worship the moon." And Solomon
   answered, "Behold!
   Little bird! if thou liest not, this queen shall the
   Merciful serve!"

SOLOMON'S SIGNET. 147

Thereafter the message went from the servant of God,
  the king:
 "Solomon, son of David, to Balkis, queen of the
  south:
Peace be to them that follow the Name upon Solomon's
  ring;
 Yield thee, and worship Allah; cursed is the idola-
  trous mouth."

Then Balkis sent him gifts, of gold bricks, yellow and
  red;
 And beautiful slaves five hundred, with amber and
  musk; and a gem
Drilled with a crooked hole, which never a goldsmith
  could thread;
 And a topaz of price, unpierced, and a diamond
  diadem.

He bade the sea-worm eat a way through the unpierced
  stone;
 And the little ant carry a thread through the ruby's
  crooked drill.
"Doth she offer to Solomon gifts?" quoth he, on his
  ivory throne,
 "We are richer than Seba's kingdom! By Allah!"
  said he, "I will

"That one of my slaves bring hither Queen Balkis'
  jewelled seat;
 Thereby she shall learn that the glory is ours, and
  the knowledge and might."
Then Asaf the wise commanded, and a Djin spread
  his pinions fleet,
 And brought the moon-throne thither, and set it before them aright.

In a guarded house she had shut it, which a thousand bowmen kept,
But when she was come to Salem, lo! Solomon the king
Sate there on her own gold seat, and Balkis bowed her and wept,
Saying, "I pray thee, teach me the Name on thy signet ring!

"We have sinned against our souls, following lower Lords;
Our kingdom we give, and our goods, and our lives, and our spirits to thine."

. . . .

Such worship had he of old who knew *Al-Wâli's* words
Which rule the rulers, and knew the sound of the Name Divine.*

---

*Ya Wâli! Gracious Lord! impart
True knowledge of Thee, as Thou art.*

---

* Cf. Korân, xxvii. chapter "Of the Ant."

77

*Praise Him, Al-Mutâhâli! Whose decree
Is wiser than the wit of man can see.*

'Tis written in the chapter " of the Cave," *
An Angel of the Lord, a minister,
Had errands upon earth, and Moses said,
" Grant me to wend with thee, that I may learn
God's ways with men." The Angel, answering, said,
" Thou canst not bear with me; thou wilt not have
Knowledge to judge; yet if thou followest me,
Question me not, whatever I shall do,
Until I tell thee."
    Then they found a ship
On the sea-shore, wherefrom the Angel struck
Her boards and brake them. Moses said, " Wilt drown
The mariners? this is a strange thing wrought?"
"Did I not say thou couldst not bear with me?"
The Angel answered—" be thou silent now!"

 Yet farther, and they met an Arab boy:
Upon his eyes with mouth invisible
The Angel breathed; and all his warm blood froze,
And, with a moan, he sank to earth and died.
Then Moses said, " Slayest thou the innocent
Who did no wrong? this is a hard thing seen!"
"Did I not tell thee," said the Minister,
Thou wouldst not bear with me? question me not!"

---

* Cf. Korân, xviii.

Then came they to a village, where there stood
A lowly hut; the garden-fence thereof
Toppled to fall: the Angel thrust it down,
A ruin of gray stones, and lime, and tiles,
Crushing the lentils, melons, saffron, beans,
The little harvest of the cottage folk.
"What hire," asked Moses, "hadst thou for this deed,
Seeming so evil?"

     Then the Angel said,
"This is the parting betwixt me and thee;
Yet will I first make manifest the things
Thou couldst not bear, not knowing; that my Lord—
'Exalted above all reproach'—be praised.
The ship I broke serveth poor fisher-folk
Whose livelihood was lost, because there came
A king that way seizing all boats found whole;
Now have they peace. Touching the Arab boy:
In two moons he had slain his mother's son,
Being perverse; but now his brother lives,
Whose life unto his tribe was more, and he
Dieth blood-guiltless. For the garden wall:
Two goodly youths dwell there, offspring of one
That loved his Lord, and underneath the stones
The father hid a treasure, which is theirs.
This shall they find, building their ruin up,
And joy will come upon their house! But thou,
Journey no more with me, because I do
Nought of myself, but all by Allah's will.

Al-Mutâhâl! Maker of men,
Exalted art Thou past our ken.

78

Praise Him, Al-Barr! Whose goodness is so great;
Who is so loving and compassionate.

PITY! for He is Pitiful;—a king
Is likest Allah, not in triumphing
'Mid enemies o'erthrown, nor seated high
On stately gold, nor if the echoing sky
Rings with his name, but when sweet mercy sways
His words and deeds. The very best man prays
For Allah's help, since feeble are the best;
And never shall man reach th' angelic rest
Save by the vast compassion of Heaven's King.
Our Prophet once, Ayesha answering,
Spake this: "I shall not enter that pure place,
Even I, except through Allah's covering grace."
Even our Lord (on him be peace!); oh, see!
If *he* besought the Sovereign Clemency,
How must we supplicate it? Truly thus
Great need there is of Allah's grace for us,
And that we live compassionate!

                          Hast seen
The record written of Salah-ud-Deen
The Sultan? how he met, upon a day,
In his own city on the public way, .
A woman whom they led to die. The veil
Was stripped from off her weeping face, and pale
Her shamed cheeks were, and wild her dark fixed eye,
And her lips drawn with terror at the cry

Of the harsh people, and the rugged stones
Borne in their hands to break her, flesh and bones;
For the law stood that sinners such as she
Perish by stoning, and this doom must be;
So went the wan adulteress to her death.
High noon it was, and the hot khamseen's breath
Blew from the desert sands and parched the town.
The crows gasped, and the kine went up and down
With lolling tongues; the camels moaned; a crowd
Pressed with their pitchers, wrangling high and loud,
About the tank; and one dog by a well,
Nigh dead with thirst, lay where he yelped and fell,
Glaring upon the water out of reach,
And praying succor in a silent speech,
So piteous were its eyes. Which when she saw,
This woman from her foot her shoe did draw,
Albeit death-sorrowful, and looping up
The long silk of her girdle, made a cup
Of the heel's hollow, and thus let it sink
Until it touched the cool black water's brink;
So filled th' embroidered shoe, and gave a draught
To the spent beast, which whined, and fawned, and quaffed
Her kind gift to the dregs; next licked her hand,
With such glad looks that all might understand
He held his life from her; then, at her feet
He followed close, all down the cruel street,
Her one friend in that city.

But the king,
Riding within his litter, marked this thing,
And how the woman, on her way to die,
Had such compassion for the misery

Of that parched hound: "Take off her chain, and place
The veil once more above the sinner's face,
And lead her to her house in peace!" he said,
" The law is that the people stone thee dead
For that which thou hast wrought; but there is come,
Fawning around thy feet, a witness dumb,
Not heard upon thy trial; this brute beast
Testifies for thee, sister! whose weak breast
Death could not make ungentle. I hold rule
In Allah's stead, who is ' the Merciful,'
And hope for mercy; therefore go thou free—
I dare not show less pity unto thee!"

As we forgive—and more than we—
Ya Barr! good God! show clemency.

79

*Praise Him, Al-Tawwáb; if a soul repents,
Seven times and seventy times thy Lord relents.*

At the gates of Paradise,
Whence the angry Angels drave him,
Adam heard in gentle wise
Allah's whisper, which forgave him:
"Go," it said, "from this fair place,
Ye that sinned; yet not despairing;
Haply there shall come a grace
And a guidance; and in fearing
Me, and following My will,
Blessed shall your seed be still." *

Know ye not that God receives
Gladly back the soul which grieves?
Know ye not that He relents
Ere the sinner well repents?
Terribly His justice burns,
Easily His anger turns. †

Spake our Lord: "If one draw near
Unto God—with praise and prayer—
Half a cubit, God will go
Twenty leagues to meet him so.

---

* Cf. Korân, ii. chapter "Of the Heifer," v. 35.
† Cf. Korân, ix. chapter "Of Repentance."

He who walketh unto God,
God will run upon the road,
All the quicklier to forgive
One who learns at last to live."

———

*Ya Tawwáb! for Thy mercy's sake,
Us to sweet peace and pity take.*

80, 81

*"Forgiver!" and "Avenger!" worship Him
By these two-names, Ghafoor and Muntakim.*

* O MEN, of dry clay moulded, as the potter moulds the
   jars;
O Djins, that We have fashioned from the smokeless
   fire of stars:
   What terror of the Lord will ye abide?

He is Lord of east and west, He is Lord of south
   and north;
And the seas obey the limits which He set them, pouring forth:
   What terror of the Lord will ye abide?

Their white pearls, large and small, are the handiwork
   of Him;
And the ships, with towering sails, by His winds and
   waters swim:
   Which terror of your Lord will ye abide?

But the earth and all her creatures shall die and be de-
   cayed;
Only the face of Allah will never change nor fade:
   Which terror of your Lord will ye abide?

---

* Cf. Korân, lv. chapter "Of the Merciful."

The face of Allah ruling in glorious array;
For all things look unto Him, and He governs day by
    day:
    Which terror of your Lord will ye abide?

Yet will He find good leisure, ye twain! ye Djins and
    Men,
To judge you at the judgment, O Clay and Flame! what
    then?
    Which terror of your Lord will ye abide?

If ye can pass His gateways, east, west, and south and
    north—
Which shut in earth and heaven—hasten ye! pass ye
    forth:
    Which terror of your Lord will ye abide?

But Life and Death enclose ye; by no way shall ye
    pass;
A fence of flame shall stay ye, and a moat of molten
    brass:
    Which terror of your Lord will ye abide?

And when the sky is rended, red like a new-ripped
    hide,
There shall be no accusing, admitted or denied:
    Which terror of your Lord will ye abide?

No yea nor nay! no questions! the sinner's brand is
    sin;
Thereby shall he be known, and flung Hell's blazing
    walls within:
    Which terror of your Lord will ye abide?

Flung by the forelock and the feet: "'This Hell existed not,'
Ye said. Now broil! and when ye thirst, drink sulphur scalding hot:"
> *Which terror of your Lord will ye abide?*

But sweet for him who was faithful, and feared the face of his God,
Are the Gardens of joy preparing, and the gates of the Golden Abode:
> *Which bounty of his Lord will he deny?*

With leafy branching fruit-trees are set those Gardens twain,
And softly the streamlets warble, and brightly the fountains rain:
> *Which bounty of his Lord will he deny?*

And the fruit of the Golden Gardens swings delicate, near to reach.
Where they rest on their 'broidered couches, hearing delightful speech:
> *Which bounty of their Lord will they deny?*

Therein are the shy-faced maidens, refraining their night-black eyes
From any save that glad lover whose joy is their Paradise:
> *Which bounty of their Lord will they deny?*

From any but that glad lover, that happy lord for whom
Their mouths of pearl rain kisses, their lips of ruby bloom:
> *Which bounty of their Lord will they deny?*

Shall the wages of righteous-doing be less than the promise given?
Nay! but by God, the Glorious, the debt shall be paid in heaven!
What bounty of their Lord shall they deny?

O man! fear Him, magnify Him;
Al-Ghafoor and Al-Muntakim.

82

*Praise Him, Al-Raûf, Just and Kind alway,
Who knoweth how He made us of the clay.*

SAY, "Lord of all, to Thee
    Goeth our road;
Require not of our souls
    Too much, dear God!
Thou wilt not! what was earned
    Thou dost defray;
And what was done amiss
    That we must pay;
But ah! be not extreme
    With what's forgot,
With error, or small sin.
    And load us not
With burdens which we cannot carry, Lord!
But favor, help, forgiveness afford."*

Tender His answers are:—
    (The "Chapter of the Star."†
Ayat the Thirty-Third): "The heavens and earth
    To Us pertain, and We
    Will deal, assuredly,
Well with the good, but with the ill in wrath.
    Yet not for each offence,
    Errors of flesh or sense,

---

* Cf. Korân, ii. chapter "Of the Heifer."
† Cf. Korân. liii.

Shall there be judgment, children of the loam!
    Our mercy reacheth far;
    We know ye what ye are,
And knew ye while ye lay clots in the womb;
    Sin, and be sorry, and amend:
Who seeketh God shall find Him in the end."

Ever-indulgent Maker! we
Praise for these words Thy clemency.

83

King of all kingdoms! only Thou art crowned,
Whose throne is heaven, and earth Thy footstool's round.

Ya Málik! Ya Kuddús! wa ya Salám!
O King! O Holy One! O Peace-giver!
Ya Aziz! Ya Muhaimin! Ya Múmin!
O Mighty! O Protector! Faithful ever!
Ya Jabbár! O Thou Sovereign, All-compelling!
Ya Mutakabbir! O Thou Lord excelling!
Exalted art Thou over utmost praise;
Accurst are those who graven idols raise
Beside Thee; unto them fall plagues and shames!
To Thee alone belong "the comely names."*

King of all kings! we celebrate
With endless praise Thy glorious state.

---

* Cf. Korân, lix. chapter "Of the Emigration."

84

O "Lord of awfulness and honor!" we
Lack wit and words in fitly naming Thee.

ALL things shall die and decay, but the kingdom of
  Allah endureth,
Changeless in honor and might, changeless in glory
  and grace;
Blessed be He who is Lord, possessed of all beauty and
  greatness;
All things die and decay; only endureth His face.*

Dhu'l jalál wa'l ikrám! thus ever
Praise we Thy Throne which fadeth never.

---

* Cf. Korân, lv. chapter "Of the Merciful," vv. 26, 78.

85

Al-Muksit ! " *Equitable !*" *make us know,*
As men have wrought, they shall be wrought with so.

THREE days before our Lord Muhammad passed,
They bore him to the mosque, where he uprose—
Painfully leaning upon Omar's neck—
The fever burning in his cheeks, his mouth
Dry with the wind of death, and that knit brow
Shadowed with Azrael's overhanging wings.
One thin hand on the mimbar-rail he laid,
Speaking sweet words of guidance, precious words,
The last which ever fell from those lit lips,
Teaching his Faithful.

     Then he gazed around,
And said, "Ye men of Mecca, where I lived,
Going and coming, testifying God,
I shall die soon; I pray ye answer me,
Is there among ye here one I have wronged?
I have borne rule, judging in Allah's name,
That am a man and sinful; have I judged
Unrighteously, or wrathfully, or pressed
Too hard in the amend? Let who saith ' Yea,'
Make his ' Yea ' good before my people here,
And I will bare my back that he may smite.
I have borne testimony for the truth,
Not sparing sinners; speak, if there be here
One visited unjustly; let him shame

His Prophet now, telling the sin I wrought
Before the assembly. I have gathered dues;
Declare if I defrauded any here
Buying or selling."

      And no answer came,
Except the sound of sobs and falling tears
From stern breasts and the eyes of bearded men,
Because our Lord would pass.

        But one arose,
A hamal, with his cord across his back
And porter's knot, who cried, "Abdallah's son!
Three drachms of silver owest thou to me
For wood I bore thee after 'Ramadhan!'"

 "Good friend, I thank thee," softly said our Lord,
"Because thou didst demand thy money here,
And not before the judgment seat of God:
Ill is it if men thither carry debts!"
Therewith he paid his debt, kissing the hand
Wherein the dirhems dropped; and so went home
To die upon the lap of Ayesha,
With glad face fixed on high, and holy lips
That murmured, "Allah! pardon me my sins!"

 O ye believers! if our Lord did thus,
Consider well! leave no unrighted wrongs
Against the ill time when the Angels come,
Monker and Nakîr, gliding through the dark,
And set ye up for question in the grave;
When Israfil his dreadful trumpet blows,
Summoning to judgment; when the skies roll back
Like a scorched scroll, and o'er the gulf of hell
Al-Sirât stretches, "thinner than a hair

And sharper than a sword," and yet to cross!
Ah, then! what good one wrought, he hath of help
Even to a date-stone; what of ill he wrought,
Of hindrance, to a date-stone; for your God
Is righteous, and the distribution just.

———

O just " Distributor!" incline
Our hearts to keep Thy laws divine.

86

*Al-Jami'h! praise "the Gatherer," Who divides
Evil and good unto their proper sides.*

YE who believe, stand ye steadfast in justice,
   Witnessing true though it be to displease;
Heed not your patrons, nor parents, nor kinsmen,
   Allah is nearer and richer than these.

Sit ye not down in the seat of the scornful,
   Hear not the tales which the hypocrites tell;
On the day when His children are folded together
   Al-Jami'h shall scatter the sinners to hell.*

*We take Thee for our Shepherd; keep
Safe in the fold Thy foolish sheep.*

---

* Cf. Korân, iv. chapter "Of Women," v. 139.

87

*We praise Thee; but no need of praise Thou hast,
Al-Ghanî! in Thy glory bright and vast.*

MIGHTY is He and forgiving.*
One soul did He first create,
Then He made therefrom a mate:
And to help man in his living,
Gave him herds, each with the other,
Camels, oxen, goats and sheep.
Think how Allah wakes from sleep
The babe, close-folded in its mother!
In three darknesses He shrouds it;
Wonder upon wonder clouds it.
He is Maker: can ye see
All these tokens and still be
Thankless? Yet, if so ye are,
Not beholden to your care
Is Al-Ghanî: self-sufficing
Lives high Allah, recognizing
Gladly all His creatures' love
In a changeless peace above.
Judge ye each for each; with God
No man bears another's load.
Unto Him is your return,
Then shall every spirit learn

---

* Cf. Korân, xxxix. chapter " Of Troops."

What it wrought, and what is due;
For He knows the hearts of you.

---

*Ah, Self-sufficing One! we seek
To praise Thee well, but words are weak.*

88

He is sufficient, and He makes suffice;
Praise thus again thy Lord, mighty and wise.

GOD is enough! thou, who in hope and fear
    Toilest through desert-sands of life, sore-tried,
Climb trustful over death's black ridge, for near
    The bright wells shine: thou wilt be satisfied.

God doth suffice! O thou, the patient one,
    Who puttest faith in Him, and none beside,
Bear yet thy load; under the setting sun
    The glad tents gleam: thou wilt be satisfied.

By God's gold Afternoon! * peace ye shall have:
    Man is in loss except he live aright,
And help his fellow to be firm and brave,
    Faithful and patient: then the restful night!

Al-Mughnî! best Rewarder! we
Endure; putting our trust in Thee.

---

* Cf. Korân, ciii. chapter "Of the Afternoon."

89, 90

Mu'htî and Mâni'h! Heav'n Thou mad'st, and Hell,
Providing and withholding—and didst well.

WHEN God fashioned Paradise,*
　Spake He unto Gabriel:
" See this place which We created,
　Where the justified will dwell."
Gabriel said, "My Lord! I swear
　By Thy glory, none of men
Ever of its joys shall hear
　But will strive to enter in."

Round about His Paradise
　God set sorrows and denials;
Laid the pathway steep and strait,
　Hard to find and full of trials.
"Look again!" God said; and he
　Looked, and came, and sadly spake:
" By Thy glorious majesty,
　Not one man will entrance make!"

Then the Lord created Hell,
　Set ablaze its ache and grieving;
Saying unto Gabriel,
　" This is for the unbelieving."

---

* Cf. " The Miskat-al-Mâsâbîh."

Gabriel looked and said, "I swear,
  By Thy splendor, not a mortal,
When of hell-fire he shall hear,
  Ever will approach its portal."

Round about those awful gates
  Allah set soft sins and pleasures;
Made the pathway broad and plain,
  Rich with joys and gifts and treasures.
"Look again," said God; and he
  Saw; and spake, "Save by Thy blessing,
O my Lord! there will not be
  One that must not love transgressing."

Lord of the two-fold roads, we pray
Lead us upon the rightful way.

91

*"Propitious" is He unto those that show
Compassion to His creatures; praise Him so.*

"No beast of earth, no fowl that flies with wings,"
    Saith the great Book, "but is a people, too;
From Allah sprang their life, and unto Him
    They shall return: with such heed what ye do!"

There came before our Lord a certain one
    Who said, "O Prophet! as I passed the wood,
I heard the voice of youngling doves which cried,
    While near the nest their pearl-necked mother
        cooed."

"Then in my cloth I tied those fledglings twain,
    But all the way the mother fluttered nigh;
See! she hath followed hither!" Spake our Lord:
    "Open thy knotted cloth, and stand thou by."

But when she spied her nestlings, from the palm
    Down flew the dove, of peril unafeared
So she might succor these. "Seest thou not,"
    Our Lord said, "how the heart of this poor bird

"Grows, by her love, greater than his who rides
    Full-face against the spear-blades? thinkest thou
Such fire divine was kindled to be quenched?
    I tell ye nay! Put back upon the bough

"The nest she claimeth thus. I tell ye nay!
　From Allah's self cometh this wondrous love:
Yea! and I swear by Him who sent me here,
　He is more tender than a nursing dove,

"More pitiful to men than she to these.
　Therefore fear God in whatsoe'er ye deal
With the dumb peoples of the wing and hoof.
　Yours are they; yet whene'er ye lift the steel

"To slay for meat, name first the name of God,
　Saying 'Bi 'sm 'illah! God judge thee and me!
God give thee patience to endure to-day
　The portion that He hath allotted thee.'

"So shall ye eat and sin not; else the blood
　Crieth against you." Thus our Prophet spake,
And Islâm doeth it, naming God's name
　Before the slaughter,—for that white dove's sake.

By those dumb mouths be ye forgiven,
Ere ye are heard pleading with Heaven.

92

Az-Zarr! "*Harmful*" *He is to them that sin*
Mocking the truth; O man! fear Him herein.

SHEDDÂD, the son of Ad, of Hadramaut,
Idolater, lord of the land and sea,
Hath it come to ye how he mocked at Heaven,
Saying the idols of the coast were best—
Sâkia that makes the rain, and Hâfedha
The Thunderer, Razek who gives grain to men,
And Sâlema, lady of life and death?—
And how he sware an oath by those four gods,
Drinking the palm-wine deep at Hadramaut,
That he would build a better Paradise
Than Allah's, and be Lord and God therein;
With earthly Houris fairer than those maids
Wrought of the musk and ambergris, who have
The great immortal breasts and black-pearl eyes;
With sweeter streams than Salsabîl,* and trees
Richer in fruit than Tooba:† this he sware,
Abiding not the judgment, nor the blasts
Of Israfil, nor weighing of the scales.
Wherefore he gave command that there be built
In Akhaf, on the hills, beyond the sand—
Within a hollow vale walled by wild peaks—

---

* A stream of Paradise.
† The Tree of Happiness, which grows from Muhammad's pavilion in Paradise.

A pleasure-house—beautiful with white courts
Of levelled marble, and in every court
A fountain, sparkling from a tank inlaid
With amber, nacre, coral; and around,
In every court, cloisters of columns carved
With reeded shafts and frontals, wonderful
For beast and bird and fish and leaf and flower.
And round about this pleasure-house he bade
A lovely garden bloom, terraced by lanes
Bosky with blossoming trees and rose-thickets,
Where hidden streamlets murmured and gold fruit
Loaded the boughs, and all the air was balm.
He gave command, moreover, that there rise
Hard by, with streets and markets, a fair town
Peopled by ministers of pleasure, and walled
With ramparts of the rose and pomegranate;
Wherethrough there led a double folding gate,
Fashioned of fragrant woods, and set with stars
Of silver, opening downwards to the vale,
Inscribed "The Paradise of King Sheddâd."

And when the house was made, and all the courts
Were girdled with the carven shafts, and cooled
With leaping fountains; and the roses, blown,
Filled the green vale with sweetness; and the town
Was heaped with grain and wine, and people moved
Busy and glad about its new fair streets,
Sheddâd set forth. A shining line of spears,
League-long, wound first upon the mountain-path;
And after them the camel-litters, decked
With silk and gold, and poles of silver, came
Bearing the Houris of his Paradise;
And next the Prince amid his lords: so clomb
The gay march up the sandy steeps, or streamed

Down the gray wadis. At the head of all
Rode one who held a flag of yellow silk,
Which had for its device, "*Amid his gods,
Sheddâd, the son of Ad, of Hadramaut,
Unasked of Allah, wends to Paradise.*"

   That night they entered at the silver gate,
Making bold cheer; and sweet the garden was,
And green the groves, and bright the pleasure-house
Lit with a thousand scented lamps, and loud
With dance and cymbal and the beat of drum.
But when the golden horse-shoe of the moon
Waned in the west, there came into the sky
Three clouds; and one was white and had the shape
Of a winged angel; one was red and burned
Across the planets like a blazing sword;
And one, thick black, gathered around the head
Of a bare hollow mountain, seamed with gaps
And caverns, wherefrom—full upon their feast—
Brake, of a sudden, flame and cataracts
Of blood-red molten rock, with pitchy smoke
Veiling the heavens, and rain of blinding dust,
All pierced by livid lightning-spears, and driven
By fierce winds, hotter than the breath of hell;
Which sucked the streams, and parched the trees, and
    dried
Life from the body, as a furnace draws
The moisture from the potter's clay, while earth
Rocked, quaking; and the thunder's vengeful voice
Rolled horrible from crag to crag, and mocked
The death-cry of those choked idolaters:
Whereof, when the sun rose, there breathed not one;
Nor any green thing lingered in the vale;
Nor road nor gate appeared; nor might a man

Say where the garden of King Sheddâd stood:
So were the ways uptorn, and that fair sin
Blotted from vision by the wrath of God.

   Yet to this day there lurketh—lost to view
Of all men, hardly found by wandering wolf,
Spied seldom by the vulture's hungry eye—
The remnant of the garden of Iram.
Deep in the wilderness of Aden, hid
Behind wild peaks, and fenced with burning sands,
The perished relics of that pleasaunce lie
Which Sheddâd made, mocking the power of God:
And one who tended camels in the land,
Abdallah-Ebn-Kelâbah, seeking there
A beast estrayed, followed her footmarks up
Into a gorge, which split a cliff in twain
From sky to sand, dark as the heart of night,
With thickets at its mouth and jutting rocks.
Therethrough he pushed, and when the light once more
Glimmered and grew, he spied a hollow, shut
In the gaunt barren peaks, with black dust strewn,
And piled with cindery crags and bladdered slag,
In midst of which lay—plain to see—the bones
Of Sheddâd's city and his pleasure-house;
All with their withered gardens, and the gate
Rusted and ruined; and the cloistered courts
Swathed in the death-drift, and the marble tanks
Choked to their brims; the carven columns fall'n
Or thrust awry; the bright pavilions foul
With ashes, and with remnants of the dead:
For Ebn-Kelâbah passed into the place,
And saw the valley thronged with carcases
Of men and women and the townspeople—
Not mouldered, as is wont, to whitened bone,

But dried, by the hot blasts of that dread night,
Unto a life in death; the skin and flesh
Yet clinging, and the robes of festival
Still gay of color; all those sinful ones
Slain in their sin even where the whirlwind struck:
So that he saw the dancers as they fell
With dancing-dress and timbrels; and the ring
Of watchers round them; and the slaves who made
Their music; and the bearers bringing wine,
Each by his shrivelled wineskin, dead and dry.
Also within the courts, lay corpses slim,
Rich-clad and delicate, with jewelled necks,
The Houris of that ruined Paradise.
The sunken eyes stared, and the drawn lips grinned
Under dead rose-crowns, and the shapely limbs
Were grown too lean for the loose tarnished gold
Of armlet and of anklet; dusty lay
Strings of dulled jewels on their shrunken breasts;
And brimmed with dust the cups were which they clasped
In stiff discolored fingers. In their midst
Sate, all a-gape, King Sheddâd, for a throne
Propped his dead form, and round the waist of it
A sword hung, in a belt of gold and silk,
Hilted with pearls and rubies. This he took—
The camel-man—and glided, terrified,
Back from that City of the Dead; and found
The night-black gorge, and groped his way, and brought
The sword and sword-hilt into Hadramaut,
Telling the dread things seen of Allah's wrath
Wrought on the misbelievers; and their streets
Wrecked, and their painted courts, peopled with dead.
Such awful end came on the men of Ad,
Who made the House of Iram; and their lord.

But no foot since hath found that road again,
Nor shall; till Israfil sets to his lips
The trumpet, and Az-Zarr will bid him blow.

———

*O Harmful unto mockers! we
Know and adore Thy majesty.*

93

*An-Noor! "The Light" that lightens all who live!
By this great name to Allah glory give.*

Of earth and heaven God is the Light.*
As when a lamp upon a height
Is set within a niche, and gleams
From forth the glittering glass, and seems
A star,—wide fall the rays of it:—
So shines His glory, and 'tis lit
With holy oil was never pressed
From olive tree in east or west.
It burneth without touch of flame,
A light beyond all light: the same
Guideth the feet of men, and still
He leadeth by it whom He will.

---

*Light of the world! An-Noor! illume
Our darkling pathway to the tomb.*

---

* Cf. Korân, xxiv. chapter "Of Light."

94

Al-Hâdî! Lord! the way is hard, and we,
Thy creatures, have none other " Guide" than Thee.

By many names and guides doth God
Lead men along the upward road;
He, unto each land under Heaven,
A prophet of its own hath given:
Hûd, Idris, Eyoob, Moses,—all
Upon the self-same Lord did call;
Seeing there is no way besides
His way, the Guider of the guides;
Nor any light to mortals known
Except Al-Hâdî—His alone.

'Tis told, nigh to a city-gate
Four fellow-travellers hungry sate,
An Arab, Persian, Turk, and Greek;
And one was chosen forth, to seek
Their evening meal, with dirhems thrown
Into a common scrip; but none
Could with his fellows there agree
What meat therewith should purchased be.
"Buy *uzum*," quoth the Turk, "which food
Is cheaper, sweeter, or so good?"
"Not so," the Arab cried, "I say
Buy *aneb*, and the most ye may."
"Name not thy trash!" the Persian said,
"Who knoweth *uzum* or *aneb?*

Bring *anghur*, for the country's store
Is ripe and rich." The Greek, who bore
Their dirhems, clamored, "What ill thing
Is *anghur?* Surely I will bring
Staphylion green, *staphylion* black,
And a fair meal we shall not lack."
Thus wrangled they, and set to try
With blows what provend he should buy,
When, lo! before their eyes did pass,
Laden with grapes, a gardener's ass.
Sprang to his feet each man, and showed
With eager hand, that purple load.
"See *uzum!*" said the Turk; and "See
Anghur!" the Persian; "what should be
Better?" "Nay, *aneb!* *aneb* 'tis!"
The Arab cried. The Greek said, "This
Is my *staphylion!*" Then they bought
Their grapes in peace.
                    Hence be ye taught!

---

*But unto us Thy changeless name
Is Allah—praisēd be the same.*

95, 96

Al-Azali! Al-Bâkî! praise to Thee
Who wast before Beginning, and will be
After the Ending. From Thy mercy came
Man's breath, and unto Thee returns the same.

AL AARÂF * saith—the seventh of "the Book:"—
In the Beginning God from Adam took
All who should be his seed, and bade them bear
Witness upon themselves, putting His fear
And knowledge in the hearts of all to bè,
As salt is set in all the waves of the sea.
A countless, nameless, throng there gathered they,
That unborn multitude; and God did say,
"Testify! Am I not your Lord?" And those
Replied, "Yea, Lord! we testify!" Propose
Never, then, Man! to say, "we did not have
Guidance;" it shall be answered, "Allah gave
With life that light which leadeth to the grave."

And in the chapter of "Ya Sin" † it saith—
Read in the Muslim's ear at hour of death: ‡—
A blast! and then another blast! and, lo!
At summons of the trumpet, all shall go

---

* Cf. Korân, chapter vii. verse 172.
† Korân, chapter xxxvi.
‡ This Sura is recited at the death-beds of Muhammedans,

Forth from their grave-beds, thronging once again
Unto their Lord; and some, in fear and pain,
Shall cry, "Woe, woe! what waketh us? Is this
God's word come true?" and some, in joy and bliss,
Shall say, "Now, praise to God! His prophets spake
Truth unto us." For all mankind shall wake
Together, at the trumpet; and shall wend
Together, to the Judgment, in the end.

And no soul shall be wronged in that dread place
For aught not wrought; nor any soul find grace
Except for what it wrought; and there shall fall
Endless delight in Paradise on all
Who kept that witness! happy they shall be
Reclining with sweet consorts, 'neath the Tree
Which bears all fruits, and groweth by the Throne.
And they shall hear the Lord say to His own,
"PEACE!"—they shall hear the Merciful say so.

But to the sinners shall be thundered, "Go!
Divide herefrom! did not ye testify?"
"Yea, dreadful Lord!"—thus shall they make reply,
Descending into Hell.

Thy mercy send,
Thou, the Beginning and the End!

97

Inheritor! all things proceed from Thee,
And re-committed to Thy hands shall be.

THE chapter of Al-Hajar:* There is nought
But from the treasury of God was brought;
   Such and so much He lends them; winds and waters;
Have *ye* the store of these things, or of aught?

Did *ye* set in the sky the starry band,
Or pile the mountain peaks upon the land?
   Verily He hath made and will unmake them,
And all these shall return into His hand.

"O Rose!" the Dewdrop said, "whence didst thou
     spring,
That art so sweet and proud and fair a thing?"
   "From dust I sprang," she said, "and ere to-morrow
Back to the dust I shall be mouldering."

"O Dewdrop!" said the Rose, "where didst thou gain
This light, that like a gem on me hath lain?"
   "A cloud," he said, "uplifted me from ocean,
And I must trickle to the deep again."

The Bulbul heard; "O Allah's rose!" it said,
"The air is fragrant with thee, being dead;
   O Allah's Dewdrop! ere the sea did suck thee,
She was the fairer; be thou comforted!"

---

* Cf. Korân, chapter xv. verse 21.

For saith the chapter of Al-Hajar: "Tell
My servants I have made the heavens well,
 And the earth well, and with a steadfast purpose;
And Paradise is Mine, and Mine is Hell."*

---

*Inheritor! all things are Thine;
Al-Warith! O Thou might Divine!*

---

* Cf. Korân, xv. vv. 49, 85.

98

Earth knows, heaven shows; the holy scriptures say,
How righteous and "unerring" is Thy way.

"WE sent it down upon the 'Night of Power,'*
  The Book which 'doth declare'
In all the year that night is best: one hour
  Thereof, in praise and prayer,

"Is worth a thousand days of joy; for then
  The Angels bear commands,
Bringing the will of Al-Raschîd to men;
  Descending on all lands.

"Peace ruleth till the rising of that dawn,
  While Allah doth ordain
How many souls those twelve moons shall be born,
  How many shall attain.

"His mercy; for the books are brought of these,
  And each account is cast;
And Allah maketh 'the allowances,'
  Accepting souls at last."

Thus spake our Lord, and Ayesha replied,†
  "O Prophet! are there none
Accepted, save by mercy?" "None!" he cried,
  By God! I say not one!"

---

* Cf. Korân, xcvii. chapter "Of Power."
† Cf. the Mishkat-el-Mâsâbîh.

THE PROPHET'S OATH.

"Not thou!—not even thou!—*thou* not to go,
  Unquestioned, into heaven,
Who walked with Allah's Angels, and below
  Taught us the message given?"—

He drew his cloth across his bended face
  And thrice he spake to her:
"Except God's mercy cover me with grace,
  I shall not enter there!"

*O Al-Raschîd! and if not he,
Increase to us Thy clemency.*

99

*O loving-kind, "long suffering" Lord! once more
We praise Thee, magnifying Az-Zaboor.*

PATIENT is Allah, and He loveth well
The patient, saith " the Book," * and such as dwell
   In kindness, asking pardon of their sins
Each dawn, and pardoning the blamable.

Islâm! this is the Faith! thyself resign,
Soul, mind, and body, to the will divine:
   The kingdom and the glory and the power
Are God's, and God's the government,—not thine!

THERE IS NO GOD BUT GOD! and He is All;
And whatso doth befall ye doth befall
   By His decree: therefore, with fear and love
Upon His glorious names devoutly call.

---

*Allah! His holy will be done!
Islâm!—we bow before His throne.*

---

* Cf. Korân, iii. v. 15, chapter " Of Imran's Family."

NOTES.

Page 15, *line* 17.—One version of this legend says that Soharah (or Zoharah) herself, the spirit of the planet Venus, descended to tempt the two Angels. Harût and Marût are fabled to be confined still in the vicinity of Babel, where a man may go to learn sorcery of them, hearing their voices, but never seeing their forms.

Page 17, *line* 20.—Gabriel, or Jibraîl, is called in Arabian theology *Rû'h-el-Amîn*, "the Faithful Spirit," or *Rû'h-el-Kuddûs*, "the Holy Spirit." It was he who delivered the Korân to Muhammad.

Page 18, *line* 3.—A commentator on this legend writes: "Some say that Solomon brought these horses, being a thousand in number, from Damascus and Nisibis, which cities he had taken; others say that they were left him by his father, who took them from the Amalekites; while others, who prefer the marvellous, pretend that they came up out of the sea, and had wings. However, Solomon, having one day a mind to view the horses, ordered them to be brought before him, and was so taken up with them that he spent the remainder of the day, till after sunset, in looking on them; by which means he almost neglected the prayer, which ought to have been said at that time, till it was too late: but when he perceived his omission, he was so greatly concerned at it, that ordering the horses to be brought back, he killed them all as an offering to God, except only a hundred of the best of them. But God made him ample amends for the loss, by giving him dominion over the winds."

Page 18, *line* 17.—Arafat is a mountain near Mecca, so named from the tradition that Adam, upon his repentance, was reunited there to Eve, after a separation of two hundred years.

Page 22, *line* 1.—Isráfíl is one of the Archangels, who will sound the last trumpet at the resurrection. He has "the sweetest voice of all God's creatures."

Page 22, *line* 13.—Iblís, "He who despairs," is Shaitân, or Satan, who fell from Heaven on account of arrogantly refusing to pay reverence to Adam at the creation, when all the other Angels worshipped the first man.

Page 23, *line* 1.—*Wuzú'h*, or washing (either with actual water, or by imitating the process with sand, etc.), must precede all those prayers which are *farz*, or "incumbent." These are commenced in a standing attitude, *Kiyám*, the thumbs touching the lobes of the ears and the face turning towards Mecca.

Page 24, *line* 9.—The "Companions of the right hand" are so called because they will have the book of their good deeds put into their right hands in token of salvation; while evil-doers will have their scroll of condemnation, at the last day, thrust into their left hands.

Page 24, *line* 13.—"Such, moreover, as of old time," etc. These are the early prophets and holy teachers in all nations. The text of the Koran calls them "the leaders, the leaders!" that emphatic repetition denoting their dignity, and the assurance of their prominence in the final reward.

NOTES. 193

Page 25, line 23.—"Mawz-trees." The original word *talh'* may mean either the plantain, or that acacia which has small round golden blossoms.

Page 26, line 1.—Sale has a citation upon these privileged attributes of the Houris. "Allah has created them purposely of finer materials than the females of this world, and subject to none of those inconveniences which are natural to the sex. Some understand this passage of the beautiful women; who, though they died old and ill-favored, shall yet all be restored to their youth and beauty in Paradise."

Page 27, line 8.—"At Azan." The time of the call to prayer, and especially after the sun has begun to decline.

Page 31, line 13.—"And spider." One of the Sûras of the Korân, the 29th, is named after this insect.

Page 32.—"The Verse of the Throne." This (which is often engraved on seal rings in the East) is so called from the word *Koorsíy*, the "chair or throne" of Allah, which occurs in the sublime passage cited. In the judgment of Muhammedans the "Throne-Verse" is one of the noblest portions of the Korân, surpassing in majesty of diction all other human compositions. It is taken from the 2d Sûra, verse 256, and is rendered very exactly, as below, by Mr. Redhouse (to whose most learned and laborious article in the "Journal of the Royal Asiatic Society," January, 1880, my indebtedness has been extremely great):

"God, save whom there is no God, is the Living, the Self-existing One. Drowsiness overcometh Him not, nor sleep. Unto Him belongeth whatever is in the heavens, and whatever is in the earth. Who is he that shall make intercession with Him, save by His permission? He knoweth whatever is before them, and whatever is behind them; and they comprehend not a single matter of His knowledge, save only that which He hath willed. His firmament spans the heavens and the earth, the preservation whereof doth not distress Him. And He is the Most High, the Most Supreme."

N.B.—Each chapter of the Korân is called a *Sûra*, a term signifying a course of bricks in a wall; and the Sûras are divided into '*âyât*, verses, or more literally "signs."

Page 33.—This Sûra, 59, is known as the chapter "Of the Emigration."

Page 34, *line* 1.—The Muslim doctors call the scriptural Terah, the father of Abraham, by the name of Azar. This was also the title of the god of the planet Mars. Abraham's father is moreover styled Zarah in the Talmud, and Athar also, by Eusebius.

Page 34, *line* 25.—"Friend of Allah." The Muslims so denominate Abraham, *Al-Khalîl*.

Page 37.—This is suggested from Sûra 35, the chapter "Of the Angels," or "Of the Originator." The Archangel Gabriel is said to have appeared to Muhammad, on the night of his journey to Heaven, having no less than three hundred pairs of wings!

Page 38, *line* 15.—"Michael," or Mikâ'îl. The Archangel here named was especially the guardian of the Jews. The Israelites of Mecca told Muhammad that they would have received his Korân, if Michael instead of Gabriel had revealed it.

Page 39, *line* 15.—"Azrâël." The Archangel of Death.

NOTES. 195

Page 40, *line* 1.—" God's Friend." *Vide* note on page 35, *line* 15.

Page 44, *line* 16.—" People of the bench." This was the name given to the poor persons whom the Prophet sustained by alms every day, and who used to wait for his gifts, sitting upon the bench outside Muhammad's house at Medina.

Page 49.—The very remarkable Sûra quoted here, entitled sometimes "The Brightness," came to the prophet thus: "It is related that no revelation having been vouchsafed to Muhammad for several days, in answer to some questions put to him by the Koreish, because he had confidently promised to resolve them the next day, without adding the exception, *if it please God*, or because he had repulsed an importunate beggar, or else because a dead puppy lay under his seat, or for some other reason; his enemies said that God had left him: whereupon this chapter was sent down for his consolation."

Page 50.—"The Journey of the Night." "It is a dispute," writes Sale, "among the Muhammedan divines, whether their Prophet's night-journey was really performed by him corporally, or whether it was only a dream or vision. Some think the whole was no more than a vision; and allege an express tradition of Moâwiyah, one of Muhammad's successors, to that purpose. Others suppose he was carried bodily to Jerusalem, but no farther; and that he ascended thence to Heaven in spirit only. But the received opinion is, that it was no vision, but that he was actually transported in the body to his journey's end; and if any impossibility be objected, they think it a sufficient answer to say, that it might easily be effected by an omnipotent agent."

Page 51, *line* 25.—"One *Fâtihah.*" The name of the opening prayer of Muhammedans.

Page 52, *line* 22.—"Monker and Nakîr" are the two Angels who conduct "the examination of the Tomb." They come to a man directly he is laid in his grave, and catechise him as to his faith. If he repeats quickly and gladly the formula of Islâm, they cause him to repose in peace; but if he is uncertain or heterodox, they belabor him with iron clubs, till his cries are so bitter that they are heard all through the earth, except by men and Djins. Then the two black Ministers press the clay down upon the corpse, and leave it to be wasted and consumed till the time of resurrection.

Page 59, *line* 15.—"'Hadîth." The traditional sayings which supplement the Korân.

Page 60, *line* 2.—"Zem-Zem." This is the holy well at Mecca, within the sacred precincts, believed to be that very spring which was revealed to Hagar when she fled with Ishmael.

Page 62.—This legend of Nimrûd is alluded to in Sûra 21 of the Korân, entitled the "Chapter of Prophets."

Page 63, *line* 19.—"Black Halîmah." The Prophet was suckled by a Bedouin foster-nurse.

Page 64, *line* 6.—"Hirâ." A wild and solitary mountain near Mecca.

Page 68, *line* 5.—"*Mîkât.*" These are the last six stages on the journey to Mecca. The *i'hrâm,* or "garb of sanctity," consists of two wrappers without seams, one bound round the waist, the other passed over the shoulders. The *tawâf* is the seven-fold circuit of the

NOTES.

Kaabah, made three times quickly, and four times slowly, by all pilgrims.

Page 73, *line* 4.—"Ye let stray your she-camels." Nothing is held more valuable among the goods of an Arab than a she-camel near to foaling.

Page 73, *line* 13.—"Who killed thee, little maid?" This alludes to the ancient practice of infanticide among the Arabs, which Muhammad strenuously denounced.

Page 74, *line* 7.—"He saw it and he heard." Alluding to the Prophet and his journey to Heaven.

Page 79, *line* 7.—"*Al-Akhâf*" is the plural of *Hekf*, and signifies "lands which lie in a winding or narrow boundary," specially applied to a district in the province of Hadramaut.

Page 82, *line* 14.—"*Al-Kâuthar*." This word signifies *abundance*, especially of *good*, and thence *the gift of wisdom and prophecy*. Or it may mean *abundance of wealth, followers*, and the like. It is here used of a river in Paradise, whence the water is derived into Muhammad's pond, of which the blessed are to drink before their admission. According to a tradition of the Prophet, this river, wherein his Lord promised him abundant good, is sweeter than honey, whiter than milk, cooler than snow, and smoother than cream; its banks are of chrysolites, and those who drink of it shall never thirst.

Page 87, *line* 2.—"*Al-Târek*" is the "star that appears" by night, *i.e.*, the morning star.

Page 89, *line* 1.—"When the soul comes to the neck." A Korânic phrase for the last gasp of death.

Page 92, *line* 20.—" The roses on that tree." In the mystic language of the East, the rose is the symbol of that Divine beauty which is the object of the soul's love.

Page 94, *line* 16.—"*Hilliyûn.*" This means literally "exalted places."

Page 95, *line* 4.—"*Tasmîn.*" A stream in Paradise, so called because it waters the highest regions there.

Page 96, *line* 12.—"*Al-Fâtihah.*" This is the 1st chapter of the Korân, which is also a prayer, and held in great veneration by the Muhammedans, who give it many honorable titles; as the chapter of *prayer*, of *praise*, of *thanksgiving*, of *treasure*, etc. They regard it as the quintessence of the whole Korân, and often repeat it in their devotions both public and private, as Christians do the Lord's Prayer.

Page 96, *line* 24.—"The morning mills." At daybreak in Eastern countries almost the first sound of awaking domestic life is the noise of the stones used to grind meal.

Page 98, *line* 6.—"The time for prayer," says Professor Palmer, "is called from the minarets of the mosques by Muezzins or criers, in the following words: 'God is great' (4 times); 'I bear witness that there is no God but God' (twice); 'I bear witness that Muhammad is the apostle of God' (twice); 'Come hither to prayers' (twice); 'Come hither to salvation' (twice); 'God is just!' 'There is no other God than God!' In the early morning the Muezzin adds, 'Prayer is better than sleep!'"

Page 101 (*note*).—"The *Mishkât-al-Mâsâbîh.*" The book of the conversations of the Prophet.

NOTES.

Page 106, *line* 7.—*Lailat-al-Kadr*, "The Night of Power," was that on which the Korân was declared to have been revealed.

Page 123, *line* 18.—"*Al-Barsakh.*" The Korân says, "Behind them shall be a bar, until the day of resurrection." Upon this Sale writes: "The original word *barzakh*, here translated 'bar,' primarily signifies any partition, or interstice, which divides one thing from another; but is used by the Arabs not always in the same, and sometimes in an obscure sense. They seem generally to express by it what the Greeks did by the word Hades; one while using it for the place of the dead, another while for the time of their continuance in that state, and another while for the state itself. It is defined by their critics to be the interval or space between this world and the next, or between death and the resurrection; every person who dies being said to enter into *Al-Barzakh*. The commentators on this passage expound it as a barrier, or invincible obstacle, cutting off all possibility of return into the world, after death."

Page 123, *line* 22.—"Birds." If the departed person was a believer, the Muslims say two Angels meet his soul, and convey it to Heaven, that its place there may be assigned, according to its merit and degree. They distinguish the souls of the Faithful into three classes: the first of prophets, whose souls are admitted into Paradise immediately; the second of martyrs, whose spirits, according to a tradition of Muhammad, rest in the crops of green birds which eat of the fruits and drink of the rivers of Paradise; and the third of other believers, concerning the state of whose souls before the resurrection there are various opinions. Some say they stay near the sepulchres, with liberty, however, of going wherever they please; which they confirm from Muhammad's manner of saluting the dead, alluded to elsewhere.

Page 131, *line* 1.—The "ten holy eves" are the first ten nights of the sacred month of *Dhu'l Hejjeh*.

Page 131, *line* 7.—"Iram" was the name of the palace and pleasure-garden built by Sheddâd, son of Ad, in the desert of Aden. The story is related on another page.

Page 131, *line* 9.—The Thamudites of the Hadramaut having killed their prophet, were utterly destroyed by tempests, and their city depopulated.

Page 146, *line* 11.—"Al-Hudhud." The Arab historians, Sale says, tell us that Solomon, having finished the temple of Jerusalem, went in pilgrimage to Mecca, where, having stayed as long as he pleased, he proceeded towards Yaman; and leaving Mecca in the morning, he arrived by noon at Sanaa, and being extremely delighted with the country, rested there; but wanting water to make the ablution, he looked among the birds for the lapwing, called by the Arabs *Al-Hudhud*, whose business it was to find it; for it is pretended she was sagacious or sharp-sighted enough to discover water underground, which the devils used to draw, after she had marked the place by digging with her bill: they add, that this bird was then taking a tour in the air, whence, seeing one of her companions alighting, she descended also, and having had a description given her by the other of the city of Saba, whence she was just arrived, they both went together to take a view of the place, and returned soon after Solomon had made the inquiry which occasioned what follows.

"It may be proper to mention here what the Eastern writers fable of the manner of Solomon's travelling. They say that he had a carpet of green silk, on which his throne was placed, being of a prodigious length and breadth, and sufficient for all his forces to stand on, the men placing themselves on his right hand, and the spirits on his left; and that when all were in order, the wind, at his command, took up the carpet, and transported it, with all that were upon it, wherever he pleased; the army of birds at the same time flying over their heads, and forming a kind of canopy, to shade them from the sun."

Page 147, *lines* 17-20.—"The sea-worm and the ant." The legend is that Solomon used the *teredo* to bore his topaz, and, by filling the winding hole of the ruby with sugar and water, tempted an ant to draw a silk thread through it.

Page 165, *line* 26.—"Monker and Nakîr." These are the two Angels who visit the dead immediately after burial, and having set them upright in the grave, question them as to their faith and actions, as before described.

Page 165, *line* 31.—"Al-Sirât." The narrow bridge which all must cross from this to the next world, "finer than a hair and sharper than a razor."

"This bridge," it is written, "is beset on each side with briers and hooked thorns; which will, however, be no impediment to the good, for they shall pass with wonderful ease and swiftness, like lightning or the wind, Muhammad and his Muslims leading the way; whereas the wicked, what with the slipperiness and extreme narrowness of the path, the entangling of the thorns, and the extinction of the light, which directed the former to Paradise, will soon miss their footing, and fall down headlong into hell, which is gaping beneath them."

"Muhammad seems to have borrowed this from the Magians, who teach that on the last day all mankind will be obliged to pass a bridge called Pûl Chînavad, that is, *the strait bridge,* leading directly into the other world; on the midst of which the Angels appointed by God will stand, who will require of every one a strict account of his actions. The Jews speak likewise of the bridge of hell, which they say is no broader than a thread."

Page 168, *line* 9.—"Three darknesses." The body, the womb, and the amnion.

Page 174, *line* 15.—This is the origin of the *Hallal,* a custom of Muslim hunters and butchers, who pronounce the formula of excuse and pity before slaying any animal.

Page 184, *line* 1.—"Al-Aarâf." The partition between Heaven and Hell. The chapter quoted says, "And betwixt the two there is a wall, and they shall cry out to the companions of Paradise, 'Peace be upon you,' but they cannot enter it, although they so desire."

www.ingramcontent.com/pod-product-compliance
Lightning Source LLC
Chambersburg PA
CBHW020330170426
43200CB00006B/339